MW01127308

From Awful to Awesome

9 Essential Tools for Effective Presentations

Don Franceschi

SPECIAL OFFER

Thank you for buying my book! To show my appreciation, please go to http://www.FromAwfulTo Awesome.com and receive a FREE downloadable workbook to supplement the tools, techniques, and tips discussed in this book.

Included in the FREE workbook are some of the forms, checklists, and chapter summary charts that can help you master those all-important 9 essential tools for effective presentations.

Did I mention the workbook is FREE?

Help support the worthy cause of saving the world from awful presentations!

http://www.FromAwfulToAwesome.com

Dedications

To my mom, Sandy ...

To my dad, Geno ...

To my son, Ean ...

To my wife, Elena ...

Thank you for always believing in me.

Disclaimer

This book is designed to provide information on effective presentations only. This information is provided and sold with the knowledge that the publisher and author do not offer any legal or other professional advice. In the case of a need for any such expertise consult with the appropriate professional. This book does not contain all information available on the subject. This book has not been created to be specific to any individuals or organizations' situation or needs. Every effort has been made to make this book as accurate as possible. However, there may be typographical and or content errors. Therefore, this book should serve only as a general guide and not as the ultimate source of subject information. This book contains information that might be dated and is intended only to educate and entertain. The author and publisher shall have no liability or responsibility to any person or entity regarding any loss or damage incurred, or alleged to have incurred, directly or indirectly, by the information contained in this book. You hereby agree to be bound by this disclaimer or you may return this book within the guarantee time period for a full refund.

Acknowledgements

I would like to acknowledge the following individuals for their contributions to my inspiration and knowledge on all aspects of effective presentations:

Darren LaCroix, Craig Valentine, Ed Tate, Patricia Fripp, Tim Gard, James Jeffley, Manley Feinberg, Maureen Merrill, and Michael Port.

A special thanks to the following individuals who contributed to this book being written:

Chaim Eyal—For your mentorship, encouragement, and book input.

Doug Ziemer—For allowing me to teach my "Effective Presentations and Public Speaking" class, which helped inspire the creation of this book.

Cate Griffiths—For your insight, sound advice, and suggestions.

Jon Lehre Graphic Design—For the book illustrations.

Carola Bartz—For the author photograph.

Elaine Roughton—For the book editing.

Angie Mroczka and Jennifer Henderson—For the book formatting and cover.

TABLE OF CONTENTS

Foreword

Given the array, and continued rush, of material about presenting and public speaking, any writer, publisher or bookseller might well pause before adding yet more to the list. A search on Amazon alone returns more than 20,000 entries. Why *does* this river of this information never cease?

On the positive side, our culture changes: today's presenter must discard many of the techniques taught decades ago. And, new research tells us more about how the brain receives, how the heart listens, and about the way messages resonate in contemporary listeners. Ideally, this section of our (paper or electronic) bookshelves would respond to that information in a big, effective way. We need resources that really support us—but also, resources that encourage us to see the value in making the commitment to extraordinary communication.

Unfortunately, most material on this topic just doesn't help. If it did, we'd have a delightful abundance of great presenters. But usually, told that we're about to hear *a presentation,* we roll our eyes and groan because we have *endured* presentations, tried to chuckle at lame jokes, and finally got happy when the phrase, "In conclusion ..." inevitably rolled around. So much "how to present" or "how to speak" lit conveys old, obvious info in a way that fails to spark passion or inspire hope. Most writers keep trying to say the same thing in a new package.

It's darn hard to speak well in public, and information isn't the only answer. We need reasons to learn, personal motivation to develop, and help in finding our personal voices. What sets this book apart is its energy, the "you-can-do-it" spirit, and the absolutely precise practical advice.

Part of the charm is that Don keeps asking, learning, and wondering as he shares the facts of good speaking in a personal, natural tone of continuing discovery. As I read along, I trust his observations and can easily see how they arise from hard-won experience. I feel that I'm in the hands of someone who's taken this path and dearly loves sharing it. His natural energy comes through as a buddy alongside you, instead of an Important Speaker dispensing wisdom.

This book moves forward, as any good presentation does—with telling details, stories, clear general principles, and specific, sometimes quirky examples. Had you thought before about the difference between practice and rehearsal, a failsafe way to minimize your use of notes, or what to do if, in an effort to "spread out," your audience begins re-arranging the room? Although the flow is smooth enough that you can enjoy this book cover to cover, you'll likely mark out many parts that you'll come back to for specific tips when you need them. There's a lot here, so have a good time with it, and don't expect to absorb everything at one sitting!

The telling details that Don provides, with humor and humanity, let us know that he cares about our success. There's a rare unselfishness in his sharing, and his determination to be sure we get it shows huge generosity. These, of course, are the qualities of great presenters.

Perhaps the whole point of communication in public is to have an impact that uplifts, informs, and inspires people to use their potential for greater things. This work achieves exactly that, and will help you do the same.

Maureen Merrill, M.A., is a speaking coach, workshop leader, and retreat facilitator based in northern California. She speaks frequently on the topics of leadership communication, volunteer motivation, customer service, and personal presence.

TAKING *"PRESENTATION ROAD"* FROM AWFUL TO AWESOME!

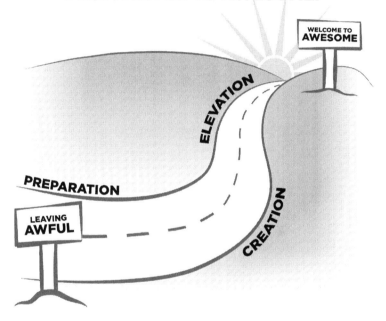

Introduction

Have you ever attended a bad presentation? Was it YOUR presentation? I feel your pain! I still remember the first, and definitely the worst, presentation that I ever gave. I was a rookie "Safety Representative" for my company. We met with policyholders and made recommendations on how they could improve their safety programs. This involved conferences, inspections, and occasionally, safety presentations.

As part of my initial training, I had tagged along with several of my co-workers and observed them in action as they performed their conferences, inspections, and safety presentations. Every safety presentation they gave was remarkably similar—about 15 minutes long, for about 10 people, and for an enthusiastic audience. Based on my observations, I made what seemed a logical assumption that these presentations were no big deal. When our department assistant relayed to all of us at a staff meeting that a request for an after-hours safety presentation had been received, I volunteered. I mean, what could go wrong?

I wish you could have been with me that night. The presentation was scheduled for 7 p.m. It was dark, pouring down rain, and I was hopelessly lost. The clock on the car's dashboard was a constant reminder that I was running out of time. Sweat was beading up on my forehead and my heart was pounding. I did NOT want to be late for my first presentation!

Finally, with just minutes to spare, I found the correct building. In a very unsafe manner, I semi-skidded into a gravel parking area and jumped out of the car. Did I mention that it was just pouring? I popped the trunk to get all of my presentation equipment and materials, and ran to the building's large oak front door. With my arms full, I struggled opening the door, and was finally able to fling it open.

Have you ever been surprised? I mean REALLY surprised? Instead of the 10 people that I expected, I found myself in a large auditorium style room with 104 pairs of eyes staring at me—in complete silence. Uh-oh! I must have been quite a sight. I was completely drenched and my hair was plastered down on my head. As I carried my equipment and materials inside, my shoes made a loud squishy-squeaky noise every step. As I set up my overhead projector, and miraculously didn't electrocute myself as I plugged it in, out of the corner of my eye I thought I caught a glimpse of steam coming off my body.

This was awful! I was positive the audience could see my heart beating through my drenched shirt. My hands were shaking so badly that I could barely place the first transparency on the overhead projector. I couldn't raise my head and look at my audience; I was fixated on that first transparency. With a throat that was feeling more constricted every second, I finally managed to generate some sound, and in a high, trembling voice, I read my introduction. "My name is Don Franceschi, and I'm your Safety Representative."

That's as far as I got. It was at that point that a young lady in the front row turned to the young lady next to her, and in a very loud stage whisper, said "Man, he's really nervous, isn't he?"

I wanted to die. As I looked at the floor, I prayed that it would open up, swallow me up, and put me out of my misery. I'm sad to say that the presentation actually went DOWNHILL from there. That was 28 years ago, and that awful experience seems like it was just yesterday. Let's fast-forward to today—you are holding my book on how to give effective presentations. What? How did that happen? How did I go from giving one of the worst presentations ever to now giving advice on making presentations effective? Well, it wasn't easy. My book is a result of many presentation classes taken, speaking conferences attended, numerous articles and books read, lessons learned from Toastmasters International and Toastmasters' contests, developing Effective Presentations and Public Speaking classes for my company, and a great deal of trial and error practice— with an emphasis on error.

I'm not special. You can certainly take the time and effort to improve your presentation and public speaking skills just like I did. However, if you are an inexperienced, infrequent, or ineffective presenter— and you would like to significantly shorten your learning curve—**this book is for you**! You will learn the nine tools for giving an effective presentation. These nine tools are divided into three sections.

Section one is PRESENTATION PREPARATION. Section two is PRESENTATION CREATION. Section three is PRESENTATION ELEVATION. Each section has tools, techniques, and tips that can assist you in giving better presentations.

Mastering these tools doesn't guarantee that every presentation that you give will be awesome. Think of this book like the seat belt in your car. Wearing a seat belt doesn't guarantee that you won't be hurt or killed in an accident, but like a seat belt, this book can greatly increase your chances of presentation survival! So jump in your car—buckle up!—and let's start the journey on "Presentation Road" from Awful to Awesome!

Section One—Presentation Preparation

Let's imagine creating a great presentation is like building a house. There is a particular order that needs to be followed to build a house correctly. You wouldn't start with constructing the roof and building down from there. (Although I would love to see that attempted!) Whether it is a house or presentation, you need to start with a solid foundation. It is my personal observation that many presenters skip over this vital stage, and the evidence is in thousands of conference rooms in thousands of locations where these "foundation-less" presentations are given. Did you attend a bad presentation today? If not today, how about in the last few weeks? It's likely that presenter didn't do the foundation work required to create a great presentation.

Why don't most people do this foundation work? I think it is because it's not something that most people are taught or aware of or are comfortable with. I recently saw a presentation exercise that brings this point home. The presenter asked everyone to stand and place both arms straight out and parallel to the floor. Then when he said, "Go," everyone was to fold their arms as quick as possible and freeze. He then asked the audience to check HOW they folded their arms—which arm was on top, which hand was tucked under, and which hand was on top. Then he asked the group to put their arms straight out again, and this time when he said, "Go," everyone was to fold their arms the OPPOSITE way and freeze. He asked if people felt a difference from the first attempt and the second attempt. Most people thought the second attempt was harder, slower, and more awkward because they had to think about what they were doing—it wasn't natural. The presenter's main point was that new ways of doing things can feel awkward at first, but over time practice makes perfect. If you practiced the opposite way of folding your arms, it would soon feel as natural and smooth as the "normal" way.

In the introduction, in excruciating detail, I outlined the worst presentation that I ever gave. I used NONE of the presentation preparation tools that I'm going to give you, and I paid the price that night. I didn't know better at the time. When you finish this section, you won't have that excuse, and you can avoid the pain that I went through during that awful presentation. Some of this foundation work might seem awkward at first, but if it's new to you, that's to be expected. Just keep at it and eventually you will get to the point where it feels natural using the presentation preparation tools. Let's get to that all-important first tool—Message.

MESSAGE

One of my least favorite activities is sitting through a rambling presentation. You know, the kind of presentation that goes on and on and on with no clear destination in sight. Recently, when I was being tortured with one of these rambling presentations, I heard the person next to me mutter under their breath, "Is this plane going to land soon?" I was thinking the same thing! There are usually two missing elements in a presentation that just meanders along. Let's focus on the first element, which is also our first effective presentation tool—Message.

What do I mean by Message? The Message in your presentation is the main idea or theme or concept or point or objective. I'm less concerned with what you call it, and more concerned that you actually have one. It's what you want the audience to take away when you are done presenting. If they only remember one thing from your talk, you want your Message to be that one thing. Sounds obvious, right? But I never cease to be amazed at how many presentations have no clear Message. This is effective presentation tool number one, so you need to master it before you go any further. Imagine that the Message is the sun, with all of the other planets (tools) revolving around it.

If you do an Internet search for "types of presentations or public speaking," you will find a wide variety of responses, but usually they include categories such as informational, educational, motivational, entertaining, and persuasive. One of my mentors, Chaim H. Eyal, PhD., of Eyal and Associates, once told me, "All communication is designed to persuade." Taking that concept further, I believe that all presentations and speaking falls under just one category, persuasive. You are trying to persuade your audience to see something in a particular way, to feel something in a particular way, or to act in a particular way. Think of your Message as a persuasive "call to action" that you can build on by using the other effective presentation tools.

Assuming that I've convinced you how important your Message is to your presentation, how do we make it an effective one?

To have an effective message, it needs to have the 3 C's. These 3 C's all work together. Your message needs to be:

- **Clear**
- **Concise**
- **Catchy**

Let's start with the first C—**Clear**. You need to be clear on what your message is. If it's not clear to you, it can't be clear to your audience. Let that sink in for a moment....

So how can we be sure that we are Clear? Step one is acknowledging that there is a PURPOSE for every presentation. Think of an iceberg:

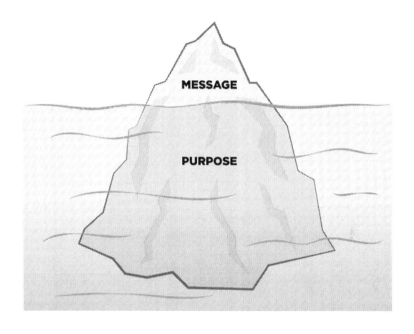

Your Message is the part that we see above the water—the tip of the iceberg—but the bulk of that iceberg that's below the water is the Purpose. I've heard the 2000 World Champion of Public Speaking, Ed Tate, say that it's important to know the KFD when you speak—what you want your audience to KNOW, FEEL, and/or DO at the end of your presentation. That's the purpose—that's what you have to be clear on because that's the whole reason for the presentation in the first place. Have you ever given a presentation where you were not entirely sure what the purpose was? Maybe you were "volun-told" to give the presentation by your boss and you were a little fuzzy on why? If this situation or something similar rings a bell with you, how did that presentation go? Were you confident, or a little unsure and tentative? Did the audience seem engaged, or were they more confused or bored? Remember—a clear purpose creates a clear message.

The second C stands for **Concise**. You should be able to state your message in 10 words or less. Why? By forcing your message to be concise, you automatically make it clearer. This is much harder to do than you might think. One of my favorite quotes along these lines was from Mark Twain. "If you want me to give you a two-hour presentation, I am ready today. If you want only a five-minute speech, it will take me two weeks to prepare." Having competed in Toastmasters speech contests, where you would be disqualified if your speech went over 7 minutes, 30 seconds, I'll vouch for Mark Twain's words.

The last C stands for **Catchy**. You want your audience to remember your take-away message. Otherwise, what's the point? Having a message that is clear, concise, and catchy can greatly increase the chances of that message being memorable. What makes a message catchy? Let's look at a few examples of what I consider to be a catchy message that I've used or heard recently. "Don't aim for perfection, shoot for connection." "Stay alive—don't text and drive." "Click it or ticket." "Don't let others shortchange you—Never shortchange yourself." "To stay insured with us, they must work with us."

As you can see from some of the examples, using rhyme or alliteration or repetition gives your message a "pop," which makes it so much easier to remember—for you as the presenter and especially for your audience.

Your turn. Think of a current topic that you could be asked to give a presentation on. It could be related to your work, or a club you belong to, or a hobby, etc. See if you can come up with an effective message using the 3 C's. Go ahead—I'll wait.

Welcome back. How did you do? When I give an Effective Presentation class, this is one of the exercises that I have folks do. Many people have told me that creating an effective message was much harder than they thought it would be. We are not used to being clear when we speak. We tend to just start talking, which leads to rambling. We are not used to creating a catchy memorable message, which leads to our rambling being instantly forgettable. In summary, "winging it" is not an effective message creation strategy. Using the 3 C's does get easier with practice, and the result is creating a foundation for a presentation that really resonates with your audience.

Though this chapter may be short, the impact on your presentation will be HUGE—don't underestimate it!

Now that you are clear on WHAT your Message is, the next step involves knowing WHO you will be giving that message to. The second Presentation Preparation tool is your AUDIENCE.

AUDIENCE

One thing that all presentations have in common is that they involve some type of Audience, which is our second Presentation Preparation tool. To give an effective presentation, you need to know and understand your audience. Again, this seems obvious, but too often presenters don't take the time to really know who they will be speaking to. Let me ask you, would you give the same presentation on global warming to a group of scientists as you would to a group of second graders? I asked that question to a class I was giving recently. They laughed, and someone from the audience said, "Of course not." When I asked, "Why not?" they replied that the audiences were so different that a presentation that made sense to one of the groups would be inappropriate to the other one. I then asked if any of them researched their audience before they gave a presentation. Not many hands went up. You can use the 3 C's to create a great message, but if you are not familiar with your audience, it will be hard to tailor that message to them and less likely you will be able to persuade them with your "call to action."

How can you research your audience so you DON'T give your global warming presentation designed for scientists to second graders? I like to start with the person that asked you to do the presentation in the first place: your boss, a co-worker, a policyholder, a client, a customer, event planner, whoever it may be.

In many cases, this initial contact person will have more information regarding your future audience than you do. If they don't, they likely can at least steer you in the right direction of who DOES have the information that you need. Assuming that we get to the right person, some of the information that would be helpful to know includes:

- What does your audience care about and why? (Knowing this can make it so much easier to connect with them.)

- Are there any particularly sensitive issues? (If so, you might want to address those very carefully during the presentation.)

- What is their experience/education level? (This can help you avoid the "scientist/second grader" issue we already mentioned.)

- What is some of the common jargon/"lingo" that the group uses? (Knowing your audience's language can make it so much easier to build a connection with them and convey your message.)

- Does the audience have a particular gender, cultural, or generational makeup that would be helpful to know ahead of time? (For example, if the average age of the audience is 23, I would approach the presentation differently than if the average age is 53.)

- Has this audience had a previous presentation that they really enjoyed? What was it about that presentation that really resonated with them?

- (You can see this one coming.) Has this audience had a previous presentation that really crashed and burned? What made that presentation ineffective for this group?

Do you see how doing this Presentation Preparation research on your audience could really be helpful? You can cherry-pick off of what has already been successful, and avoid what has been proven not to work for this group. In addition, I would ask if there are a few audience members that would be good candidates for contacting ahead of time that you could interview. I know, I know, some of you are thinking, "Well, how many is a 'few'?" That really depends on the answers that you receive to the above questions. If the group is more homogenous, you might get all the information you need from contacting two or three people. If the group is more mixed, with varying levels of experience/education for example, then I recommend that you increase the size of your contact group.

Before speaking to these future audience members, it's great if your initial contact person could give them a heads-up that you'll be reaching out to them. If you can meet with them in person, that's great. The second best choice is on the phone. I don't like to use email for these interviews because I've noticed that many folks will be more candid in person or on a phone call than they will be in writing. When I do conduct the interviews, I like to keep them short and sweet. After telling them what the presentation will be about (this is where your message comes in) I ask them three main questions:

- What are their issues and concerns regarding the topic that I should know about? (Find the pain points. Your initial research should have given you a taste of what these are, but there is no substitute for actually checking directly with them.)

- What do they hope to get out of this presentation? (WIIFM—What's In It For Me— knowing this can help you tie your message to their concerns.)

- What would a successful presentation look like to them?

I grant you, there is some overlap between these three questions, so sometimes there is some overlap with the answers. Generally though, I have found that some variation of these three questions usually gets me the information that I need, without taking up a lot of my interviewee's time.

IMPORTANT NOTE: Take a second look at that message that you created to see if it now needs to be "tweaked" in some way.

If a particular presentation situation doesn't lend itself to interviewing some future audience members, you can still research your audience by checking the company or department website, newsletter, etc. They can often provide useful and helpful information that you can utilize during your preparation.

Another helpful way to research/profile your future audience is by utilizing a Behavioral Style analysis such as the DISC method. This is a more advanced technique, and I go into this in a lot more detail in the BONUS section at the end of this book—be sure to check it out.

At this point, you've nailed down your Message (what you are going to say), and you have researched your Audience (who you are going to say it to.) That leaves us with WHERE you are going to say it. The last Presentation Preparation tool is STAGE.

STAGE

I mentioned my worst presentation in the Introduction. I would like to say that was the only bad presentation that I've ever given, but unfortunately that wouldn't be accurate. Another one of my less than stellar presentation attempts occurred when I was scheduled to discuss several safety topics at a remote sawmill on a hot summer day. I had brought a visual aid for this talk, a safety film. (Yes, I know I'm dating myself here.) I lugged my bulky and heavy film projector and screen (Why make two trips?) to the designated outbuilding where the meeting was going to take place. The sawmill employees hadn't arrived yet, so it looked like I would have a few minutes to get ready. I set up the projector screen, set up the film projector, and put the round film reel on the front projector arm and partially threaded the film into the projector. I would have to turn the projector on to finish the process, so I grabbed the power cord and went to plug it in.... Uh, where is the outlet? I searched high and low on every wall—I couldn't find an outlet. As the first sawmill employees started to enter the room, they began laughing at me. "This building has no power. How are you going to show a film?"

Oh boy. These were some of the toughest-looking guys that I had ever seen, and they were all laughing at me. I asked the supervisor if we could use another building that had some power. "This is the only room big enough to fit everyone in," he told me. I said I'd be back in a minute, and I ran to my car in the parking lot. I prayed that I had some safety materials that I could hand out to replace the film that I wasn't going to be showing. Luckily, I did have some material to hand out on safe lifting, so I had to change what I was going to discuss on the fly and was forced to give an abbreviated safety presentation, on a topic I wasn't as familiar with, as sweat rolled down my face from my run to the car and my nervousness. The supervisor, taking pity on me, not only helped me get through the presentation but also helped keep his crew under control.

You can know your message, you can know your audience, but if you don't know your stage your presentation can go downhill fast.

The Stage is the physical location/setting for your presentation. I include the equipment that you will be using under this definition as well. What are some of the Stage issues that can affect a presentation? When I ask my audiences, some of the typical answers are as follows:

- Room too hot/cold

- Room is the wrong size for the group

- Room configured awkwardly

- Wait staff interrupting your talk

- Missing items (Such as the flip chart, markers, etc.)

- IT issues (PowerPoint not working, projector not working, no power, microphone not working, etc.)

This is obviously not an all-inclusive list, but I've attended meetings where one or more of these issues helped sink a presentation. I bet you have too. Before we get more specific, there are two general solutions that will solve many of these stage issues. They are:

1. **SCOPE OUT THE ROOM AHEAD OF TIME.** My definition of "ahead of time" is at least a day before your presentation. It's amazing how few people actually take the time to do this. By doing this you get to verify how the room looks, what equipment is available, and how the room is or can be set up. Now I'm sure some of you are thinking, "I can't scope out the room ahead of time." Maybe you can't get to the location before your presentation. This happened to me recently. I live in Santa Rosa, California, which is about 60 miles north of San Francisco. I was asked to give a presentation at our organization's Monterey Park office in Southern California. I had never been there before. What to do? Well, everybody has a smart phone now, and I asked some colleagues that worked in that office to take some pictures of the conference room and send them to me. Specifically, I asked for pictures

from the audience's point of view facing the front of the room, from the speaker's point of view facing the audience, pictures of the overhead projector, the projector screen, and lastly, pictures of where my laptop would go along with the connection outlets for power and to access the projector. It sounds like a lot, but those five or six pictures gave me a wealth of information. I could see the size of the room and the type of tables and chairs being used, which let me plan out in my head how I could set the room up. I was able to see that there was space at the front of the room for my laptop, electric outlets were readily available next to the connection for the projector, and even that there was a separate cable for accessing the room's speaker system. I verified that flip charts were available to use, and the photo of the room from the speaker's vantage point allowed me to visualize giving my presentation there, which made me more comfortable the day of the presentation because it felt like I had been there before. Scoping out the room ahead of time physically is a best practice, but if you can't do it physically, then at least have photos or videos of the room sent to you as a next-best alternative.

2. **ARRIVE EARLY.** Have you ever attended a presentation where the presenter waltzed into

the room a few minutes before the presentation was scheduled to start, and then frantically tried to rearrange the room, or get their laptop set up, or get their materials ready to go? Did this delay the start of the presentation? As an audience member, weren't you thinking, "Why didn't he/she take care of this BEFORE I arrived?" I admit that this is a pet peeve of mine. It's disrespectful of your audience's time to not be set up and ready to go at the scheduled time. So arrive early. It will allow you to set up the room the way you want, or to verify that the room WAS set up the way you want. If there are any temperature issues, you can have them addressed by the appropriate folks as soon as possible. You will be able to make sure that your equipment, such as a laptop or projector, are hooked up and working properly. If the room has an overhead projector, it will allow time to locate the remote control for that projector, which always seems to go missing the day of the presentation. You will have time to arrange your flip chart(s) the way that you want, have your flip chart markers out, and have any handouts or other materials ready to go. You get the picture— arriving early allows time for all of these things to get done. Most importantly, it gives you time to "get centered" before the presentation so you are able to give your audience your full attention right from the start.

Again, those two general solutions will address most issues regarding your stage, but in case they don't, let's get more specific.

- Room too hot/cold—Knowing who to contact for "climate control" is very important, as many conference rooms either have the thermostat adjustment locked up, or it is controlled from outside the room. Even if you arrived early and the room temperature was fine, there is no guarantee that it will remain fine for your presentation, so be sure to have that contact information. If you are able to request a specific temperature, between 70 and 72 degrees seems to be the sweet spot for most folks. Having worked as a Property Manager for my company at one point, I fully realize that no one temperature will make everyone happy. Based on that Property Manager experience though, that 70 to 72 degree range definitely reduced the number of temperature-related complaints that I had to deal with. I will also suggest that it's better to err on the side of having the room be a little too cool rather than a little too warm. People can put on a sweater or jacket if they are cold, but most situations don't allow for removing clothes if you get too hot. Plus, a room that is too warm definitely affects the audience's ability to pay attention, wouldn't you agree? (Interesting tidbit: while I was proofreading this section of my book, I heard a news report that listed a Republican Presidential Debate requirement that the room temperature not go over 67 degrees. Granted that requirement was for the debate participants—not the audience—but I did find it interesting.)

- Room is the wrong size for the group (too small)—I'm going to assume that you were able to scope out the room ahead of time and were unable to move to a larger room. If you are stuck with the room, your main option is to see if you can break the presentation into two or more sessions. It can be miserable for your audience to be crammed into a room. That much body heat in a small room can overwhelm the HVAC temperature setting, and as mentioned in the previous point, it's hard to pay attention when you can feel the person next to you sweat. Gross. The only other option I've used in this situation is to significantly shorten the presentation—I just hit the highlights and got them out of there. Don't prolong their misery—your audience will be grateful, I promise you.

- Room is the wrong size for the group (too large)—I've had this situation much more frequently than having a room that is too small. The biggest problem here is that people tend to spread out all over the room, with most folks in the back as far away from the presenter as possible. They want to be able to talk to their friends, play with their phone, and if they can get away with it, catch up on their sleep. The result of all of this "spread-out-ness" is that the audience's energy is diffused throughout the room instead of being concentrated in front of you. The simple solution I use is to set up the room the way I want it ahead of time, and take away or move the excess tables and chairs. (This is one of the reasons I arrive early.) It's harder for folks to spread out if they don't have any place to spread out to. You still have to be vigilant—I had a group at one presentation that started to reassemble the room set-up so they could sit a mile away from me in the back. I politely, but firmly, stopped the attempted room reconstruction. This is YOUR presentation, and you are in charge, so take charge.

- <u>Room configured awkwardly</u>—Often, adjoining conference rooms can open up a dividing wall and create a larger room. Sometimes this can create problems because now there may be pillars or columns that you have to work around. Other times, the tables and chairs may have not been set up the way you requested or expected. (Another reason to arrive early.) Which leads to a question that some of you might be thinking, "Is there one best way to set up a room that works every time?" Quick answer—nope. There really isn't a perfect setup that works every time for every presentation. However, I have come up with three simple rules that can guide you:

Rule #1. Everyone needs to be able to see you.

Rule #2. Everyone needs to be able to hear you.

Rule #3. Keep any exercises or activities that you are planning in mind.

To check the first two rules, I try to sit in all four corners of the room beforehand. Will the audience member in that seat be able to see me? Will they be able to see the screen if I'm showing a PowerPoint presentation or a video? Will they be able to see my flipchart? If someone can stand in the front of the room speaking while I'm doing this, it will also allow me to determine if I can be heard in all four corners as well. Then I review any exercises or activities that the audience will be doing. If folks will be coming up to the front, is there easy access? If we will be breaking up into smaller groups, how can I set up the room to make that easier to do? You get the point. If everyone can see you, hear you, and participate in any activities or exercises easily, then the room is set up correctly.

- <u>Wait staff interrupting your talk</u>—I've been involved with many presentations that were either held in restaurants or were in a main conference room where they were serving a meal. Many professional speakers have it written into their contract for the event that the servers will be out of the room during their presentation. Why do they do that? Because it is human nature to be easily distracted, and food being served or tables being cleared is a distraction. Although you might not be a professional speaker, we can learn from their example and try to at least minimize the amount of distraction that occurs. This will require coordination between the meeting planner, the restaurant event coordinator, and yourself. Each situation will be different, but generally you want the wait staff to go about their work before or after your presentation— just not during. It's not always possible, and if it's a "working lunch" or similar type of meeting, some interruptions might be unavoidable. If you were able to make some arrangements ahead of time to avoid distractions, it is up to you to stick to the agreed time schedule in fairness to the restaurant's staff—they have a job to do, too.

- Missing items—One of the reasons to arrive early is to locate missing items, such as that AWOL flip chart, and/or markers. I swear these items must grow legs at night because they always seem to have wandered off before your presentation. If you will be writing on a white board, be sure that you are using the right markers, because regular flip chart markers tend to not wipe off—which is a problem. (Ask me how I know that!) There have been times where I actually did have my own spare flip chart in my car when I have driven to a presentation—but that option is clearly not available all the time. I do have a supply of markers—flip chart and white board markers—that I bring to the presentation as a backup.

- IT issues—Last, but definitely not least, we come to the generic "IT issues" category. Just as you need to know who your "climate control" contact is, you also need to know who your IT contact will be. I know I'm beating this to death, but as indicated earlier, arriving early allows you time to get your laptop set up properly, the projector working properly WITH the remote control, microphone check, room sound system check, laptop remote control check, etc. Let me give you a real world example. I was giving a presentation that my boss was going to sit in on, and I definitely wanted everything to go smoothly. I followed my own advice and scoped out the room the week before. During that visit, I wanted to make sure that I knew how to hook my laptop up to the overhead projector. There was already a room laptop that was connected, so I put my laptop on the other laptop, moved the connections to my laptop and verified that everything was working great. The day of the event, I again put my laptop on the other laptop—but this time I couldn't get my PowerPoint to come up on the projector. I restarted my computer—still nothing. I have to admit that my forehead started getting a little damp. I called the IT contact person—and got their voicemail that they were out of the office for the day. I couldn't believe it. As I was shaking my head in disbelief, I took a look again at my laptop that was sitting on top of the room's laptop. I noticed that all of the connections were connected like they were supposed to be—however, they were still connected to the room's laptop, not mine! I hadn't moved them. What a bonehead—no wonder nothing was working. I moved the connections to my laptop and, thankfully, everything worked perfectly. By arriving early, it allowed me time to be a bonehead, and more importantly, solve the bonehead problem I created. If I had arrived just before the presentation and had made the same bonehead mistake, I probably wouldn't have figured out what I had done wrong before I had to start— and I wouldn't have been able to show the PowerPoint or videos during the presentation like I wanted to do.

On all issues regarding your Stage, a good thing to remember is that if you can make a change—make it. If you can't—acknowledge it and move on. For example, if the room is too hot, don't stand there with sweat running down your face and pretend that there is no issue. You may think that by ignoring the situation, your audience will ignore it as well. It doesn't work that way. What is actually running through the audience's mind is, "Oh, I'm dying here ... I'm roasting ... why isn't something being done to fix this ... I'm miserable...." If these thoughts, or something similar, are running through your audience's mind—and this is the PG version of their thoughts—then you HAVE to address the situation, because they won't listen to anything else that you have to say until you do. For example, you might say, "I've notified the building engineer that the room is too warm. He is working to fix the problem. If I receive an update from him, I will let all of you know." And then, move on with your presentation. By acknowledging the situation, you help diffuse it. By moving on, you help deemphasize it. Again, if you can make a change—make it. If you can't—acknowledge it and move on.

Your Message. Your Audience. Your Stage. Hopefully, by now you see the value of these three Presentation Preparation tools. In my awful first presentation story in the Introduction, I didn't use any of these tools. I didn't really know what I was going to say, didn't know anything about who I was saying it to, and I didn't even know where I was going to be saying it. Three strikes and you're out. That presentation was doomed before I said my first word. I didn't know better at the time. Now you do. Learn from my mistakes—for the sake of your audiences, please don't repeat them. Let's recap the highlights from this section before we move into Section Two— Presentation Creation.

MESSAGE

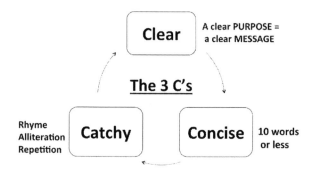

AUDIENCE

To connect with your audience—you first need to KNOW your audience

Research your audience ahead of time with your initial contact person

Determine their issues--experience/education levels-- "lingo" & makeup

Interview future audience members--Keep it short and sweet

Behavior Style analysis can help you profile your audience ahead of time

STAGE

Stage issues can sink a presentation

Two general solutions for most stage issues--

#1--Scope out the room ahead of time

#2--Arrive early

Stage issues (part 1) If you can make a change, make it

Stage issues (part 2) If you can't —acknowledge it and move on

Section Two—Presentation Creation

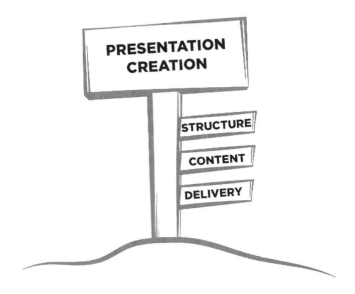

Now that you have an understanding of the Presentation Preparation tools—that foundational work—it's time to actually create the presentation itself. If Message is WHAT you are going to say, Audience is WHO you are saying it to, and Stage is WHERE you are saying it, then the three tools in this section all determine HOW you are going to say it. The three Presentation Creation tools are Structure, Content, and Delivery. Each of these tools builds on the others. Your presentation needs a framework to work with (Structure). You need to fill that framework with your thoughts, knowledge, and examples that support your Message (Content). Finally, you need to communicate that Content to your Audience (Delivery).

Let's get started!

STRUCTURE

I mentioned earlier how much I dislike rambling presentations, which are usually a result of two missing elements. We've already identified the first missing element—lack of a clear, concise, and catchy Message. The second missing element is our first Presentation Creation tool—Structure.

If you think of a presentation like a person's body, then Structure would be the skeletal system. Without all 'dem bones, humans would be just be a big pile of Jello. Structure in a presentation helps shape and define it. If it's missing, then the presentation is just a big pile of a non-Jello substance, if you get my drift.

There are many different presentation structures out there. So, which is the best? Honestly, most of the different presentation structures I've seen or used have been some variation of the most basic structure of all—a Beginning, a Middle, and an End. That's pretty basic, isn't it? However, believe it or not, I've attended many presentations that didn't have one or more of these elements, and I bet you have too.

You might be thinking, "I already knew that my presentation needed to have a Beginning, a Middle, and an End. This isn't helpful." Fair enough—if we were going to just stop there. However, let's discuss in detail what goes into each one of these elements so we can transfer those general words into specific meanings and actions.

Presentation Structure

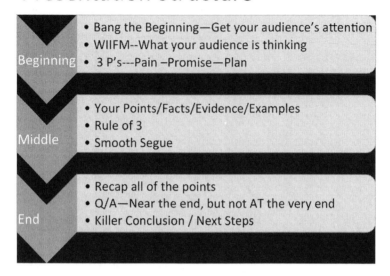

Beginning
- Bang the Beginning—Get your audience's attention
- WIIFM--What your audience is thinking
- 3 P's---Pain –Promise—Plan

Middle
- Your Points/Facts/Evidence/Examples
- Rule of 3
- Smooth Segue

End
- Recap all of the points
- Q/A—Near the end, but not AT the very end
- Killer Conclusion / Next Steps

BEGINNING

There have been many studies that show that an audience decides pretty quickly whether they are going to mentally participate in a presentation or tune you out. Some studies indicate that you have to make an impact within the first five minutes. Other studies have stated that you have approximately one minute to get your audience's attention. I recently heard of a study that dropped that time down to seven (7) seconds! Wow! Regardless of which study is the most accurate, the one fact that all of the studies confirm is that as a presenter you have a limited window of time to get your audience to tune in and not tune you out. That means that we need to BANG THE BEGINNING. In this fast-paced, distraction-rich environment that we live in, we need to generate an emotional response with the first words out of our mouths. Do most presentations do that? No. Let me give some examples of opening lines that I've heard presenters use recently, along with a quick commentary:

- "Well, I guess we should get started." (Guess again—the presentation has ALREADY started. And we are not exactly starting with a bang, are we?)

- "This isn't an exciting topic, but we have to go over it." (Many times a significant portion of your audience wishes that they didn't have to be there. This statement indicates that YOU don't want to be there either.)

- "Has everyone signed in?" (Boring announcement.)

- "I'm really not good at giving presentations." (Let me ask you—does this inspire confidence in the presenter? Does this make you glad you're in the audience?)

- "The bathrooms are out the door and to the right." (Boring announcement.)

Do any of these introductory phrases ring a bell? Have you ever used any of these phrases or something similar? Excuse me for raising my voice for a moment, but PLEASE DON'T START YOUR PRESENTATION WITH THESE PHRASES EVER AGAIN! Good Lord, we just established that you have a limited time to get the audience's attention—maybe just seven (7) seconds—and you are going to waste those precious seconds discussing where the bathrooms are?

Now I know that some of you are thinking to yourself, "I have to tell folks to be sure to sign in or where the bathrooms are. I don't have a choice." I get it. Sometimes you do have boring announcements that you have to make—just DON'T make them the first thing out of your mouth. As far as the other phrases go, there really is no excuse.

So how SHOULD we start a presentation? Here are some better options:

- Ask a question. ("Have you ever attended a bad presentation? Was it YOUR presentation?")

- Tell a story. (My story in the Introduction would be an example. We'll discuss stories more in the CONTENT section.)

- Use an interesting quote. (My general contractor dad once told me, "Destruction is easier than construction." He also said, "It's okay to make a mistake. Just don't make the same mistake over and over again.") Don't use a quote that everyone has heard in your opening—be original.

- State a surprising statistic. ("60% of confined space deaths occur to would-be rescuers.")

- State a shocking statement. ("If a plane crashed and all 100 people aboard died, it would front page news across the country. Yet that many people die in automobile accidents every single day, and nobody seems to notice—nobody seems to care.")

All of these options are better than the typical presentation opening that you have seen. Helpful tip— no matter which of these options you choose, take a look at your MESSAGE from the Presentation Preparation section and make sure that the option is in support of that message. It needs to be related.

Now that you have your audience's attention, don't waste it. As mentioned earlier, in every presentation, the audience is thinking WIIFM (What's In It for Me). You need to address the audience's WIIFM as early as possible. How? Well, we talked about the three C's earlier for creating your Message. Now for the second stage of the Opening you should think of the three P's. They are:

- Pain
- Promise
- Plan

The first P stands for Pain. People are generally driven to take action for two specific reasons—to avoid pain or gain pleasure. Think about it. In the last 24 hours, have you done anything specifically to avoid pain or gain pleasure? I know I have. In my experience, avoiding pain is the greater motivator. If we have done our Presentation Preparation homework on our Audience, we should have an idea of their issues and concerns (their pain) regarding our message. We don't want to ignore it, we want to use it. Heck, if we can embellish the pain, even better. Why? Because we want to persuade the audience that we can help them avoid that pain.

The second P represents your Promise. This is where you tell the audience what they will take away from your presentation. In other words, you are promising to offer solutions to make their pain go away. Often this Promise is where you can state your clear, concise, and catchy Message that you have already created.

The third P stands for Plan. This is where you outline HOW you are going to accomplish all of this. Think of it as a roadmap to guide them to their final destination.

Let's use an example to better illustrate how this Beginning section works. When I give an Effective Presentations class, the first thing I do at the beginning of the class is ask a question—"Have you ever attended a bad presentation? Was it YOUR presentation?" Then I dive into my story about my first and worst presentation ever. (If this sounds familiar, I used the same question and story for the introduction to this book.) This beginning accomplishes two things right off the bat. For one, the question and the story that immediately follows start the presentation with a bang. Second, it immediately stokes a fear that most of my audience has, which is the pain of giving a disastrous presentation. Next, I make a Promise to them that when they walk out of the classroom, they will have the tools for giving effective presentations. At this point, on a flip chart, I show them my Message, which is:

MORE TOOLS = MORE OPTIONS = MORE SUCCESS.

The last thing I do for my Beginning is to explain HOW we are going to accomplish this—in other words, the Plan. "You will learn the nine tools for giving an effective presentation. These tools are divided into three sections: PRESENTATION PREPARATION. PRESENTATION CREATION. PRESENTATION ELEVATION...." You get the point. I've gotten my audience's attention, identified their fears and pain points, promised them a solution, and laid out how the solution will be presented. I'm now ready to move to the next stage of this presentation structure.

MIDDLE

Your points. Your facts. Your evidence. Your examples. Whatever you want to call them, this stage of your structure is where they go. This is where you support your message and back up the promise that you just made. In our next Presentation Creation tool, we will discuss in detail what type of audience "hooks" you can use to make your points more effectively. Each of these points should have their own mini-message that supports the overall message of the presentation.

How many points, facts, evidence, or examples do you want for this Middle stage? We are going to use the RULE OF 3 to guide us. Are you familiar with the RULE OF 3? To put it simply, people tend to learn and remember information best if it's broken down into groups of three. Retention and understanding start dropping significantly if you have more than three points.

Once you become aware of it, you will see the RULE OF 3 everywhere, and I do mean everywhere:

- Entertainment: The Good, the Bad, and the Ugly; Three Days of the Condor; Sex, Lies, and Videotape; The Three Stooges; Huey, Dewey, and Louie; Goldilocks and the Three Bears; The Three Little Pigs; The Three Musketeers

- Religion: Father, Son, and the Holy Ghost; The Three Wise Men; Heaven, Purgatory, and Hell

- Government: Executive, Legislative, and Judicial Branches

- General Phrases: "Life, Liberty, and the Pursuit of Happiness;" "On your mark, get set, GO;"

"Gold, Silver, or Bronze;" "Stop, drop, and roll;" "Morning, noon, and night;" "Three square meals a day;" "The Fire Triangle;" "Food, water, and shelter"

If it's good enough for The Three Stooges, it's good enough for me! You may have noticed that I've used the RULE OF 3 extensively in this book—I have three sections (Presentation Preparation, Presentation Creation, and Presentation Elevation) and each section has three tools in support of it. Right now we are discussing a Presentation Structure model that has three sections—a Beginning, a Middle, and an End. So, bottom line, let's not fight it—the RULE of 3 works.

Assuming that you are on board with using three points, facts, pieces of evidence, or examples to support your main Message, how do you move from point to point? Well a boring way would be to say "... and now for my second point ... and now for my third point...." We can do better than that. I like to use what I call the SMOOTH SEGUE. Let's imagine that our presentation is like driving a car to a particular destination. We are on a freeway called "Point #1." We need to get on the nearby freeway called "Point #2." If we try to turn anywhere we want, we'll crash the car. However, if we slow down at a freeway interchange and exit "Point #1," we can then smoothly and safely enter and merge onto "Point #2." A smooth segue between our points in a presentation is like a verbal cloverleaf—we slow down to recap the mini-message as we simultaneously leave (exit) one point and begin (merge) onto the next point. To do this, we can use language such as:

"As we just discussed ..." (mini-message #1), "however, we also should be aware of ..." (mini-message #2 intro)

"Now that we have established ..." (mini-message #1), "let's move on to ..." (mini-message #2 intro)

"In addition to ..." (mini-message #1), "we should also consider ..." (mini-message #2 intro)

I realize that these examples might not work for your specific presentation, but I hope that the SMOOTH SEGUE concept is one that you will utilize between your points, facts, evidence, or examples to make your presentation smoother and easier to follow for the audience.

Now that we have made our three points, it's time for the last presentation structure stage, appropriately titled the:

END

Our first step at this stage is to very briefly RECAP all of our points that we have made. Repetition helps people learn, so don't be afraid to make those points again. Once the RECAP is completed, we move to the dreaded Q&A section. Not every presentation has to have a Q&A section, but in many situations a Q&A section is appropriate. A word of advice: it's ok to put the Q&A section near the end of the presentation. Just don't put it at the VERY end of the presentation. Why? I'll use a personal example to illustrate. I was giving a presentation to about 30 of my employees at a staff meeting. The presentation was going great: the beginning rocked, the middle couldn't have gone better, and then I came to the end. I did a brief recap, short Q&A, and then moved to my conclusion. The energy in the room was awesome. Then I blew it. I asked if there were any last questions. Bam! A crazy question came at me from left field. I managed to answer it—but then it generated an even crazier question from right field. Did you ever blow up a balloon as a kid and slowly let the air out? That's what happened to my presentation—the energy in the room deflated right in front of me. I was so mad at myself. I knew better and did it anyway—Arghhhhh! Audience members tend to remember what they hear first and what they hear last in a presentation. You want the last words that they hear to be YOUR conclusion in YOUR words with YOUR message. You let the air out of your presentation if you do the Q&A at the very end of the presentation—so DON'T DO IT!

We have made it to the very END. Just like we BANGED THE BEGINNING, we need to have a KILLER CONCLUSION. Be sure not introduce any new topics at this stage—it should be a wrap-up of what you have already gone over. All of the ways that we used to open the presentation are still available to us for the End (ask a question, interesting quote, surprising statistic, shocking statement, tell a story). If we told a story at the beginning, and if there is an epilogue to that same story, that can be a very effective way to end the presentation. No matter what content you use for your KILLER CONCLUSION, be sure to include some NEXT STEPS for your audience to take. Remember, we said earlier that all presentations and public speaking involves persuasion—you want to persuade your audience to take some type of action. You don't want your information to go in one ear and out the other. Chaim Eyal told me once, "If you tell people specifically what to do, they will be more likely to do it." Sounds obvious, but too many presenters don't specify the next step they want their audience to take. Don't make that mistake—be specific.

I once heard Hall of Fame Speaker and World Class speaking coach, Patricia Fripp, say, "Last words linger." As already mentioned, people tend to remember what they heard first and last in a presentation. So make those last words memorable.

Now that we have that presentation structure skeleton in place, it's time to add some flesh and blood. To do that we need to move to our next tool—CONTENT.

CONTENT

As a presenter, we always want to have a connection with our audience. The fastest and most effective way to do that is to connect on an emotional level. This is important because, as well-known consultant, speaker, and author Alan Weiss, PhD, puts it, "Logic makes you think, emotion makes you act."

I love that quote! It really resonates with me. Facts and data ARE important, but too often we overwhelm our audience with them and leave the emotional "hook" out of the equation. For example, imagine that you are watching your favorite TV show when a commercial comes on for your local Humane Society. The screen displays a bar chart comparing the number of animals that have been adopted with the number of animals that still need to be adopted. It's all factual, accurate data. But let me ask you—does it compel you to rush out and adopt one of the animals? If you are like most people, probably not. However, what if the commercial showed a cute puppy all alone in his cage looking at the camera with his sad puppy-dog eyes? Which commercial would be more likely to motivate you to adopt an animal? I'm guessing the puppy dog one would be more effective, because it tugged at your emotions. We want to engage our audiences emotionally to create a greater connection with them, which in turn drives them to action. For the CONTENT that we put in our presentation

STRUCTURE, it's important that we emotionally "hook" our audiences by any M.E.A.N.S. necessary.

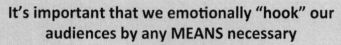

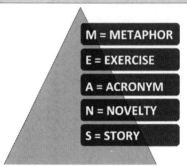

The "M" stands for Metaphor. The typical definition of a Metaphor is comparing two dissimilar items, objects, or ideas. For public speaking and presentations, our definition is a little different. We use Metaphors to compare something that is familiar or relatable to your audience with something that is not. For example, in the last tool, Structure, I compared the human skeletal system with the structure of a presentation. In that same section, I also compared driving from one freeway to another with having a Smooth Segue between the points in your presentation. In both examples, my goal was to take an idea or item or concept that most people understood well to give better understanding to an idea or item or concept that they were less familiar with. Metaphors can be wonderful additions to your presentations as long as you keep the following rules in mind:

- Don't mix your metaphors. That usually happens when you combine two or more metaphors in a way that just doesn't make sense. For example, "We will need to tighten our belt or we will sink like a rock." (Comparing hunger to drowning.)

- The purpose of using metaphors is to give clarity. You need to make sure that your metaphors are relatable to your audience. (This is where your Audience research comes in.) You wouldn't use IT terms in your metaphor to a non-IT audience, or poker references to an audience that has never played, etc.)

The "E" stands for Exercise. These would be exercises and activities that "up the energy" in the room and literally get the blood flowing. An example would be the "folding your arms as fast as you can" exercise that I mentioned earlier. As another example, in my Effective Presentation class, I have each person come up to the front of the room and state their name, their department, and their years with the company, and their favorite movie of all time. Having people participate in Exercises and physical activities not only can reinvigorate your audience, (especially if they have been seated for a while) but it also can help connect easier with your audience members that are kinesthetic learners. A couple of helpful tips:

- To avoid chaos, you need to be extremely clear with your instructions BEFORE you begin. You do not want to lose control of your presentation. Tell them exactly what you want them to do, and if appropriate, demonstrate it yourself before you have them do it.

- As part of these instructions, be sure that you have a way set up ahead of time to regain their attention when you are ready to move on. I like to ring a small bell. I tell them that when they hear the bell to instantly stop talking and to give me their attention. For a rowdy group, I even have them practice. I ask them to turn to their neighbor and talk, but stop when they hear the bell. I usually offer them a challenge, like "the last group took 5 seconds to get quiet—can you beat that?" I know this sounds a little "elementary school," but I've had good success with those more rambunctious folks using this approach.

- We will discuss the importance of rehearsing your entire presentation in a later chapter, but it is VITAL to rehearse any exercises or activities ahead of time—preferably at the location of the presentation. You can do this as part of the "scoping out your STAGE ahead of time" process that we went over earlier.

The "A" stands for Acronym. Acronyms are one type of mnemonic device that assists people in remembering information. I'm using one right now—talking about ways to emotionally "hook" our audiences by any M.E.A.N.S. necessary. Using Acronyms can make it much easier for your audience to remember that hook, and the bait—I mean point—that is attached to that hook. It's not just easier for the audience—Acronyms make it easier for the presenter to remember key points as well.

The "N" stands for Novelty. Our brains are wired to remember things that are unusual and out of the ordinary. Regardless of what M.E.A.N.S. hook you are using for your content, don't use a commonplace one that everyone has heard or done before. Let me use a totally unrelated example to make this point. Many, many years ago (did I mention many?), at my outdoor 8th grade graduation event, right in the middle of the ceremony, a masked man appeared out of nowhere, threw a pie in the face of the Principal, and ran off. Decades later, I ran into an old elementary school classmate, and the first words out of her mouth were, "Do you remember the Principal getting the pie in the face at our graduation?" That was over 40 years ago, and both of us were able to recall all the details of that moment. Why? Because this was a novel event. As a spectator or participant, I have attended dozens of graduation events over the years. However, there was only one graduation where someone was hit with a pie, and that's why it is the only one that is stuck in my memory. Now let me be clear—please don't hit an audience member with a pie! You do want people to remember your presentation, but let's not start a food fight or get arrested to accomplish that. You get the idea: most presenters don't take the time to come up with novel content to get the audience's attention and to make that content memorable. If your content stands out, so will your points. (A side benefit is that you will stand out too!)

The "S" stands for Story. I saved the best for last. In my opinion, stories are one of the most effective ways to communicate any point that you are trying to make. Way back in the MESSAGE section I stated that all presentations and speaking should be categorized as persuasive—you are trying to persuade your audience to see, feel, or act in a particular way. Using stories is the best way to accomplish that. From ancient times to modern "TED talks," stories have a proven track record of effective persuasion. Stories can bring data and statistics to life, and they can definitely help build that emotional connection with your audience that you are striving for. There are many different types of stories that are available to use, but my bias is towards personal stories. In 2014 I attended the National Safety Council Congress & Expo in San Diego. I will never forget one of the keynote presentations by Phoenix Safety Management President, Charlie Morecraft. Years before he had been involved in an industrial accident, and he was horribly injured with severe burns over 50% of his body. As he related his personal story of what led up to the accident and its aftermath, I diverted my attention from his riveting story to glance around the audience. I was sitting in the last row of this enormous conference room—I was so far back it would have been hard to see him on stage if it wasn't for the huge monitors hanging down from the ceiling. I had heard the expression, "I was sitting on the edge of my seat," but I had never seen an audience where this was actually true. I'm terrible at guessing the size of a crowd, but if I had to guess, there must have been at least two thousand people in this room, and while he shared his story, you could literally have heard a pin drop—I've never seen anything like it. It was so powerful.

Let's step back for a moment. Charlie is a Safety Expert talking to a room full of Safety Professionals. He knows his audience. He is an accomplished public speaker. His keynote would have been good no matter what his content was. However, it was his personal story that made his talk so powerful. That's the takeaway: a story, especially a personal one, can take your presentation to a much higher level.

Quick pulse check: So far in this Presentation Creation section we have discussed how you can Structure your presentation, and the type of Content that we should place in that Structure. It's time to move to one of the most important effective presentation tools—DELIVERY.

DELIVERY

Delivery is how you communicate your information to your audience. Most people would think this tool is first. When you think about effective presentations, delivery is what comes to mind for most people. Why is delivery the sixth tool instead of the first? Because if you use those first five tools it makes your delivery so much easier. You might have heard about the 55%, 38%, 7% communication rule. This rule supposedly states that 55% of communication is from your body language, 38% is your tone of voice, and only 7% is the actual words you use. I've been in several communication classes over the years where they mention this 55%-38%-7% rule. Unfortunately, this rule is based on an incorrect understanding of a study UCLA psychologist Dr. Albert Mehrabian and his fellow researchers did in 1967. This actual study was narrowly focused and not intended to reflect all types of communication. Darn!

DELIVERY

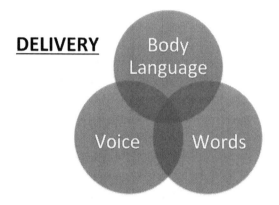

Although these widely reported percentages are not accurate for all communication, let's not toss out the baby with the bathwater. Obviously your body language, your voice, and your words DO have an effect on how your communication is perceived, so let's review each of those separate components and realize that the correct percentage weighting will vary based on the specific communication situation. Let's start with body language.

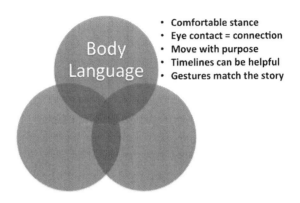

- Comfortable stance
- Eye contact = connection
- Move with purpose
- Timelines can be helpful
- Gestures match the story

Does nonverbal communication, our body language, really have an impact on our audience? Let me answer by first asking a question. Have you ever played poker or watched a poker tournament or high-stakes cash game on TV? Then you're probably familiar with the term "poker tells." Good poker players are able to analyze their opponent's body language to help them determine whether they have a strong poker hand or not. In other words, their opponents are often communicating the strength of their hand without saying a word, even when they TRY not to do so. Their body language is giving them away.

How about another example closer to home? Have you been able to read the body language of someone close to you, say a family member or friend, and know what they are thinking or feeling? Have you had that same person say one thing even though their body language was saying something else? Which did you believe? Body language is part of how we communicate, so let's look at how we can use that to add value to our presentations and not detract from our message. Let's start with a general principle. It's better to not have anything between you and your audience—so don't camp out behind the lectern. I know that the physical setup of the room and the presentation itself might not allow you to be front and center, but it's easier to establish that audience connection. So I highly recommend it when you can.

Next, let's discuss the stance. You want to stand with your feet comfortably apart, weight evenly balanced. Stand up straight, arms down at your sides, relaxed. From an audience's point of view, this looks natural. From a presenter's point of view, it doesn't feel natural at all.

Tip: If you talk with your hands a lot—like I do—you can make the arms feel more natural down at your sides by lightly pressing your index finger and your thumb together. It gives your hands something to do and it really works. Now, especially for the guys, remember to keep your hands out of your pockets. Don't jingle your coins or your keys—that's generally not the area you want your audience to focus on.

Eye contact is one of the best ways to make a connection with your audience. Something I learned from Chaim Eyal: When you look up, it means you are thinking. When you look down, it means you are lost. Really try to avoid looking down. When you make eye contact with one of your audience members, hold it for a couple seconds. However, you don't want to engage in a prolonged stare down with someone. That will make everyone feel uncomfortable, and let's face it, it's just creepy. Two to three seconds seems to work best. Eye contact with one specific person is especially effective while you are making one specific point. Be sure to move your gaze around the room because it conditions people to wait for the next eye contact, and helps build that audience connection.

One thing that I've learned from the 2001 World Champion of Public Speaking, Darren LaCroix, is to move with purpose on the stage. Too many presenters either stay rooted to one spot or wander aimlessly side to side. The "wanderers" remind me of those ducks at a shooting gallery at the county fair. Movement is only good if it has a purpose. One way to accomplish this is to use a timeline on the stage. Are you familiar with that? Please see below:

Timeline

| Oldest Dates (Audience's Left) | More Recent Dates/Today (Center Stage) | Today/Future Date (Audience's Right) |

Just like a timeline that you may have seen in a book, a timeline on stage goes from oldest dates on the left to more recent dates on the right. This is left to right from the audience's perspective, not the presenter's perspective. For example, if you are talking about something that happened in the past, you would stand to the audience's left. If you are talking about something that is happening now, you move to the center of the stage. If you're talking about what will happen in the future, you would end up to the audience's right. This works best if it is subtle. Just a couple of steps can visually make the point.

Tip: When you finish your timeline point, use transition language while you transition to the next timeline spot on the stage. Some transition phrases that I like to use are, "Let's fast-forward to ..." "Let's move ahead to ..." "Imagine it's (date in the future)."

Lastly, make your body language congruent with your words. If you are telling a story and say you were surprised—step back. If you say you are talking to a child, lean or crouch down like you would in real life. In other words, don't retell a story—relive it. Be in that moment, and have your body language and gestures flow naturally. That will add "punch" to your words and make that story come to life for your audience.

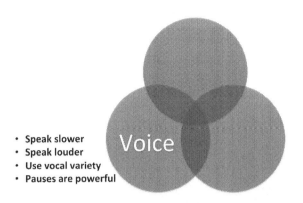

- Speak slower
- Speak louder
- Use vocal variety
- Pauses are powerful

Voice

Now that we have discussed how to more effectively communicate using your body language, let's discuss the importance of your voice. As a presenter, your voice is a critical component to making your presentation effective. Common sense, right? Let's start with what several speaking coaches have told me are the two main problems that their clients have— they speak too fast (rate) and too quietly (volume). Giving presentations make many people nervous. When you are doing an activity that makes you nervous, you usually want to get it over with as quickly as possible. Have you sat through a presentation where the speaker's voice sounded more like an auctioneer than a presenter? How about a presentation where the speaker was so soft-spoken you only caught every other word?

The solution to these two main problems isn't rocket science—you need to speak slower than you want to do, and you need to speak louder than you want to do. Some of you might be thinking, "Duh, but how much slower and how much louder?" Answer: To have a better connection with your audience, think conversation instead of presentation. Imagine you're having a conversation with one of your audience members sitting in the back, and you have to speak a little slower and a little louder so that he or she can both hear and understand you. Also, just like a normal conversation, you want to be sure to use vocal variety. A monotone "Buehler, Buehler" vocal delivery style will put your audience to sleep, which is usually not conducive to giving an effective presentation.

Remember, I said vocal variety. Have you attended a presentation where the presenter was too animated and enthusiastic for the entire time? (I'm thinking of my last car shopping experience.) Isn't that exhausting to listen to? Whether it is all monotone or too over-the-top, your presentation ends up sounding like hitting one note on the piano over and over again. That's not music to anyone's ears. The most neglected part of the presenter's delivery is actually when your voice goes silent. I'm referring to the pause. When you make a point—pause. Let that point sink in for your audience. That pause accomplishes two positive things. Number one, it allows the audience time to reflect on your point. Learning takes place during reflection. Number two, it adds to the vocal variety we are aiming for. It's a "pattern interrupt," which gets the audience's attention.

Don't believe me? For your next presentation I challenge you to stand in front of the audience—look them in the eye—and don't say a word for at least five seconds. I guarantee that you will have your audience's attention before you say a thing. I've seen the 2000 World Champion of Public Speaking, Ed Tate, use this technique very effectively.

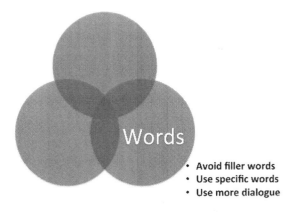

- Avoid filler words
- Use specific words
- Use more dialogue

We have discussed the effect of body language on communication and the effect of your voice on communication, now it's time to discuss the actual words that you are using and their effect on communication. Let's begin with words you shouldn't be using at all—filler words. These are the "ums," "ahs," "likes," "you knows," "sos," "okays," etc., that distract from a presentation. This is a very common problem. I attended a presentation recently where the presenter kept saying, "Okay," every few words. I caught myself starting to tally each one that I heard. In approximately 20 minutes the speaker had said okay 64 times! I happened to glance at the person on my right and noticed they were keeping track of the "okays" also.

Tip: If your audience is tallying your filler words while you speak, they are not really listening to your message. In two out of the three Toastmasters Clubs I belong to, one of the meeting functionaries is the "'ah' counter." Their job is to record those filler words— what they refer to as crutch words—and report at the end of the meeting. The first step in solving a problem is recognizing that you have one. In my Effective Presentation class, I have an exercise where teams of two take turns speaking and listening, with the listeners being the "ah" counters. Many people are shocked to hear how many filler words they routinely use. All right, you are now aware that you're using filler words, now what? Try this: When you would normally use a filler word, try using a pause instead. As we have already learned, pauses can be very effective when you are speaking.

We not only shouldn't use filler words, we also shouldn't use meandering words. What are meandering words? They're general, non-specific words that keep you from being direct and to the point. For example, don't say, "Now I'm going to tell you...." Just tell them. Imagine that you have to give someone in your audience a dollar for every word you say while you are presenting. Can you get the same message across in fewer words and save yourself some money? In the section on Message I shared the three C's. The second C was concise. I'm going to repeat the Mark Twain quote I used: "If you want me to give a two-hour presentation, I am ready today. If you only want a five minute speech, it'll take me two weeks to prepare." I'm not Mark Twain, but I like to say, "The more words you subtract, the greater your impact."

What words should we use, then? Let's start by making them specific. When we use specific words, our presentation becomes much more powerful. For example, I've heard Patricia Fripp express her disdain for speakers using words such as "stuff" or "things." Those words give no descriptive values. Don't say, "We are going to go over lots of stuff today." Try, "In the next 45 minutes you will learn the three tools you need to handle irate customers." Which of these sentences is more powerful? Also, don't forget to use your audience's profile, as you will want to use the words, phrases, and terminology that match your audience. Speaking their "lingo" will help you build a stronger connection with them.

Lastly, you want to tell your stories in an effective and engaging way since they are such a vital component of your presentations. To do that, you need a mix of narration and dialogue. Let's define those terms.

Narration is directed to the audience, is usually past tense, and could best be compared to a news report. An example of narration would be, "The cop came out of his squad car and walked slowly over to me." Dialogue is directed to a character in the story. It is present tense, like it is happening right now. Instead of a news report, think of a Broadway play. A dialogue example would be, "Son, do you have any idea how fast you were going?" When telling a story you need a mix of both, but most presenters use too much narration. Let the dialogue drive the story and make it come alive.

How can we control the nerves rather than having the nerves control us?

We have discussed the three methods that we use to communicate with our audience: our body language, our voice, and our actual words. However, we have left out one crucial component of delivery: your nerves. Using the five previous presentation tools that we have discussed will have you better organized, better prepared, and should give you much more confidence when you step out onto your stage to begin your presentation. However, it is likely you will still have some nerves. If it's any consolation, I've heard several highly paid professional speakers confess that they still get nervous. How can we control the nerves rather than having the nerves control us?

The first thing to remind yourself of is that your audience is rooting for you. Honest. They don't arrive for a presentation hoping it's horrible. "Man, I hope this presentation sucks!" They are NOT thinking that—they WANT you to succeed. If you can remember that, it does take some of the pressure off. Another "pressure reliever" is to remember that your focus should be on your audience—concentrate on them because it's about THEM, and not about you.

Over the years I've made an interesting discovery. I've noticed that somewhere around the two-minute mark, my nerves seem to disappear. I call it the "Two Minute Rule." My pre-presentation routine is to get me through those first two minutes. I start between 10 and 15 minutes before the presentation to get rid of my nervous energy. I like to find a secluded spot, which generally turns out to be the nearest restroom. I like to shadow box for maybe 30 seconds, bouncing up and down on my toes while I throw some punches. One suggestion: make sure the restroom is empty before you do this. It can be a little hard to explain to someone coming out of a bathroom stall! (I'm speaking from experience here.) Next, I do a last minute mirror check to make sure I'm presentable while taking several deep breaths. I breathe in for five seconds—hold for five seconds—then breathe out for five seconds. The shadow boxing gets some blood flowing and burns off some nervous energy, and the deep breathing helps get me centered.

When I return to the meeting room, I try to greet the attendees as they enter. I want to have a connection with them, and there is no reason that I can't start building one even before the presentation starts. I make special note of anyone that appears to be receptive and friendly, because they are good people to engage your initial eye contact with at the beginning of the presentation.

Thirty seconds before I start, I focus on my first sentence, and who I'm going to look at while I'm saying it. (Usually one of the receptive and friendly people that I identified at the beginning.) I take a last deep breath, exhale, and walk as confidently as I can to my speaking position, hit my spot, and stop—pause and scan the audience, then look at my "friendly face" as I say my first line, purposely saying it a little slower than I want to, and a little louder. I continue with my opening, and like clockwork, I can feel my nerves start to leave, and within those two minutes they are no longer an issue.

Whether your pre-presentation routine looks like mine or is completely different really doesn't matter. The goal is to have a routine that helps you get into the flow of your presentation as soon as possible so you can control the nerves, rather than having them control you.

We have come to the end of the PRESENTATION CREATION section. Let's do a brief recap of the three tools that we discussed by taking a second look at the following charts:

STRUCTURE

Presentation Structure

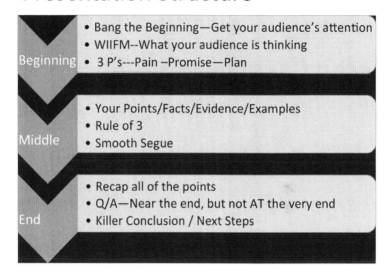

Beginning
- Bang the Beginning—Get your audience's attention
- WIIFM--What your audience is thinking
- 3 P's---Pain –Promise—Plan

Middle
- Your Points/Facts/Evidence/Examples
- Rule of 3
- Smooth Segue

End
- Recap all of the points
- Q/A—Near the end, but not AT the very end
- Killer Conclusion / Next Steps

CONTENT

It's important that we emotionally "hook" our audiences by any MEANS necessary

- M = METAPHOR
- E = EXERCISE
- A = ACRONYM
- N = NOVELTY
- S = STORY

DELIVERY

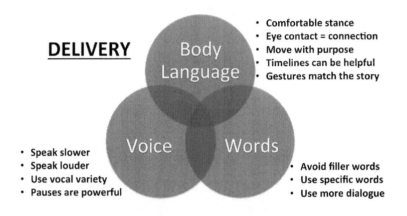

DELIVERY

Body Language

- Comfortable stance
- Eye contact = connection
- Move with purpose
- Timelines can be helpful
- Gestures match the story

Voice

- Speak slower
- Speak louder
- Use vocal variety
- Pauses are powerful

Words

- Avoid filler words
- Use specific words
- Use more dialogue

Section Three—Presentation Elevation

You've given the presentation. Whew! You've used the Presentation Preparation and Presentation Creation tools. Now what? Well, if there is any chance that you may have to give another presentation—and let's face it, there is always that chance—then this section will help elevate your presentation effectiveness to an even higher level.

The tools for this section are Review, Rehearsal, and Resources. Are we giving an effective presentation? How do we evaluate the effectiveness (Review)? If a presentation is like a performance, how can you best prepare for it (Rehearsal)? Lastly, what information is out there that can assist you in further improving your presentation skills (Resources)? Let's answer all of these questions in the Presentation Elevation section, where we "raise the bar" on what you can accomplish!

REVIEW

Whether you are a novice or an experienced presenter, it's likely that sooner or later you will give a presentation that doesn't go as well as you hoped. It happens to everyone. However, there are some presenters who are consistently awful. You know the ones I'm talking about—the folks who have a well-earned reputation for being ineffective. Why? Why do they just crush the life out of their audiences day after day, month after month, year after year?

You have all heard the famous quote by Einstein that "Insanity is doing the same thing over and over again and expecting a different result." Awful presenters remain awful because they don't change the awful things that they're doing. Why should they? I'm sure some of them think they nailed their presentation. I hate to burst their bubble, but the only way to know if you did nail that presentation is to use our first Presentation Elevation tool—Review.

Let's begin with the first type of Review that we should be doing on a regular basis for every presentation—obtaining Feedback.

FEEDBACK DURING THE PRESENTATION

When people say "feedback," they often think of it as audience input AFTER a presentation is completed. We'll talk about that "post-presentation" feedback in a minute, but first we need to focus on the feedback that you are receiving from your audience DURING your presentation. I've heard it referred to as "doing a pulse-check on your audience." Just like in life, if your audience has no pulse, it's not good. How can you determine if they are still with you? Well, let's go for the obvious first—are they involved and engaged? Are they maintaining eye contact with you? Are they actively listening? Are they participating in your exercises and activities? The answers that you receive will give you a good indication of that unspoken audience feedback.

If you have an audience where you are unclear on where you stand with your pulse check—some audiences are hard to read—what I like to do is check with some select folks during any breaks. I ask them questions like, "What did you get out of the last section," or "What parts of the presentation so far have you liked the best and the least?" You'll notice these are open-ended questions, which require an open-ended answer. I admit that I used to ask more "one-word answer" type questions in the past, like, "How is it going?" If I had a buck for every time someone said, "Fine," I'd have the money to buy that new laptop I've been eyeballing.

A presentation requires two elements—an audience AND a presenter—so be sure to take your own notes during the presentation on what you feel is going well and what isn't. For example, I had an exercise that I led where it was obvious I needed to explain the setup better. I had planned out the setup ahead of time, and was sure my instructions were clear—however, the audience gets the final say on whether you are being clear or not. It would have been easy to forget the problem I had the next time I tried that exercise or something similar if I hadn't jotted it down. Don't interrupt the rest of your presentation to write a long note to yourself—one or two words will suffice to remind you later.

During the presentation, you can also have a designated undercover "spy" in the audience who can give you some real-time feedback on specific items that you want them to focus on. Recently, I gave a presentation when I was coming down with a cold, and my voice was feeling a little strained. I knew from scoping out the room ahead of time (Stage!) that the acoustics in the room were awful and it had a loud HVAC system as well. I had my spy sit in the back row and asked him to give me a subtle thumbs up if he could hear me okay and a subtle thumbs down if I needed to speak louder. I visually checked in with him several times and was glad I did, because towards the end of the presentation my voice volume started to drop. I wouldn't have realized it if my spy wasn't looking out for me.

FEEDBACK AFTER THE PRESENTATION

As promised, let's now discuss feedback that you receive AFTER the presentation. It's typical after many presentations for the audience to complete an evaluation survey. Most of the ones that I have seen usually have a rating section and a comments section. The rating section asks the audience to rate various statements. Let's look at an example:

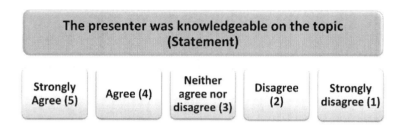

If you "Strongly Agree" with the statement, you would circle that option and the statement would receive a score of 5. I understand why Learning and Development Departments or Meeting Planners or Supervisors might want to have this type of survey scoring—it gives a numerical value that can quantify effectiveness. However, as a presenter, I honestly don't find a numeric average to be very actionable. If I receive an overall score from everyone in my audience of 5, then I probably did a pretty good job. If I receive an overall audience score of 1, then I probably did a pretty bad job. But the score doesn't give me a lot of information on WHAT I did to earn all 5's (so I can repeat it) or WHAT I did to earn all 1's (so I can improve on it). If I give two presentations back to back, and my average overall audience score is 3.9 for the first presentation, and 4.2 for the second presentation, did I actually do marginally better the second time, or did a couple of people accidentally misread the rating key and circle the wrong rating? (I've had that happen to me more than once.)

I've always found more value with the comments section of the evaluation surveys. These narrative answers usually do provide feedback that I can work with to improve my presentation. I once received feedback that when I walked into the audience during one exercise, folks had to swivel around in their chairs so they could see me. At that point I weighed the benefits of that audience interaction with the downside of some of the audience members having to move around. I decided that since the exercise only took a few moments and was an effective way to make my point, I would keep it in, but I would let the audience know ahead of time that on occasion they might have to move or turn around to follow the action. That little warning, done in a light way with a smile, made the exercise a non-issue in future presentations.

In addition to the evaluation survey that is completed at the end of the presentation, there are also email surveys, for example through Survey Monkey or some other system, that are sent to the participants within a few days of the presentation. They generally have a very similar format to the surveys that we just discussed, and with the same pluses and minuses. The down side to doing an email survey is that by sending it after the fact, the optional nature of completing the survey becomes even more optional to the recipient. If some of your participants are field employees, they might not even get to the survey for some time, and when they do, it now becomes a low priority item for completion.

Although surveys are the official "formal" way to evaluate your presentation, informal methods can provide even more valuable information. When your presentation is over, you might have folks come up to you afterwards to give their feedback directly to you. Again, don't settle for a "great presentation" comment (as nice as that is to hear), but ask, "What did you enjoy the most?" or "What's your biggest takeaway from today?" Those open-ended questions really give you more concrete information that you can actually work with.

If you had some select individuals that you checked in with during any breaks in the presentation, those folks would be good to do an audience "debrief" with now that you are finished. TIP: If you researched your audience ahead of time and conducted audience interviews, checking in with those same folks at the end of the presentation (or as soon as possible) will let you know if you utilized the information obtained from that initial interview successfully or not.

REVIEWING THE FEEDBACK

Now that you have received some feedback, you might be asking yourself, "What do I do with it?" To get a world-class speaker's opinion on this, I conducted an interview with James L. Jeffley, who was a finalist in the 2014 AND 2015 Toastmasters World Championship of Public Speaking®. In the REFERENCES section of this book, I'll discuss more about Toastmasters and their contests, but for now let's just say that being a finalist in this contest for two years in a row is an incredible feat. I've had the opportunity to see James in action on a few occasions, and he is the real deal when it comes to public speaking.

I wanted to know how James separated out valuable feedback from feedback that is "less than valuable." To paraphrase a comment I heard from another Toastmasters legend, 2001 World Champion of Public Speaking Darren LaCroix, everyone in your audience is qualified to say what they saw and what they felt during your presentation, but not everyone is qualified to coach you on what to do differently. Do you see the distinction? I loved how James threaded the needle between the types of feedback that he receives.

James said, *"I consider all input, from all sources (experienced speakers, professional speakers, non-speakers, etc.) I consider what is being said and who is saying it. I may give more credence to input from someone with more experience, but not necessarily. I will generally separate feedback into two categories: 'Impact' and 'style.' Impact is about what the audience saw, heard, and felt. I want to know how my message, delivery, energy, etc. 'landed' with them. Were they inspired, motivated, provoked to thought or action, etc.? Style is about how someone else may have done a thing. Perhaps they would have chosen a different word, body movement, gesture, facial expression or organization of the content. Maybe they would have used a prop(s). While I'm open to suggestions regarding style, I usually take these with a grain of salt, as what works well for others may not work well for me, and vice versa."*

Tagging on to James' comments, you can't act on everybody's suggestions regarding your presentations. For starters, sometimes the suggestions received are contradictory. ("You need to move more on stage," versus "You need to quit moving so much on stage.") Other times, as James said, the suggestions might not be authentic for you—and audiences will be able to tell and it will hinder making a connection with them. I heard Chaim Eyal once say about feedback that he gave to students in a class, "Take the feedback that resonated with you—leave the rest." I call it the "buffet analogy." It's good advice to follow.

Over the years I have made an observation—the folks who incorporate presentation feedback the best are also the ones who GIVE the best feedback to others. Isn't that interesting? The skills required to evaluate someone's presentation fairly, honestly, and kindly seem to be the same skills required to take feedback and make it work in an authentic way for themselves. If you belong to Toastmasters, at some point in a typical meeting you may be assigned the role of Evaluator for a specific speaker. The responsibilities of that role could include items such as reviewing the project the speaker is speaking on, and also checking with the speaker beforehand to learn about any areas they would like the evaluator to focus on. Lastly, the Evaluator usually reports to the group with their comments. This report needs to be done in a positive manner on what the speaker did well and what they could improve on. I happen to belong to three Toastmasters clubs that are blessed with tremendous talent in evaluating speakers. I feel I've become a better speaker just by listening to speaker evaluations and incorporating those suggestions in my own speaking.

If you don't belong to Toastmasters, you can still practice your evaluation skill in a modified way. For example, if you have a co-worker who will be giving a presentation, ask them ahead of time if you could work on your evaluation skills and evaluate their presentation, and then meet with them privately after the presentation to review your notes. I would ask them to explain what the purpose of the presentation is, and any specific items (talking too quickly, for example) they would like you to focus on. During their presentation, take notes on what you thought went well and what you thought could be improved. Be sure to include the items that the presenter wanted you to focus on. When you meet with them privately later to discuss, you might want to try an evaluation method that I've heard referred to as the "sandwich approach." That is, start and end with what they did well—and sandwich in the middle what they could improve upon. Use positive language even when offering suggestions. For example, don't say, "The section on the year to date results sucked." That's not helpful advice. If YOU received those comments, would YOU find them helpful? Rather, try saying, "I was confused during the section on the year to date results. If you had broken up the results by quarter, the information would have been easier to understand." Make sense? Give the feedback in the same way that you would like to receive YOUR feedback after one of YOUR presentations.

There is another way to review your presentation—you can record it.

RECORDING THE PRESENTATION

"Record your speech and it will teach." (There's a Message statement from me to you!) I try to record all my presentations whenever possible. Most of those recordings are audio recordings, as frequently the stage or the situation doesn't allow for a video recording. One of the best investments that I ever made was buying a small digital recorder. Being able to replay the presentation is very helpful in reviewing its effectiveness. We do have to acknowledge one thing, though—pretty much everybody hates how their voice sounds. I know I do. Just grit your teeth and keep on listening because the information that you are receiving is worth the pain.

I use the digital recorder a couple of different ways. If I'm able to place the recorder in an inconspicuous spot where it will pick my voice up and the audience as well, that's my first preference. Then I can just turn it on and forget about it until the presentation is over. Be sure you hit "record" and not "play" though. For a Toastmasters speech one time I accidentally hit play, and after my presentation began I suddenly heard a faint voice that I thought was coming from someone's cell phone. In my head I thought, "How rude!" I was a little distracted from my presentation. It took a few minutes before I realized that it was MY voice coming from my recorder from one of my practice sessions— the rude person turned out to be me!

For better sound, I have also used a clip style omni-directional microphone that I can put on my shirt, which picks up my voice much better. (Since it's omni-directional, it also picks up the audience.) The main negative is that I've knocked the microphone off my shirt more than once with one of my gestures, and putting it back on takes me out of the flow of my presentation.

When I play back the audio of my presentation, I always hear some "gems" and "germs" (as we call them in one of my Toastmasters clubs) that surprise me. For example, one germ that I became aware of the first few times I recorded myself was how many filler words I was using. I still haven't eliminated them, but awareness has resulted in a significant reduction.

Gems are equally helpful—I recall one presentation where I made an offhand comment that was a big hit with the audience, but I couldn't remember how I set up the comment or the exact words that I used. Playing back the recording solved those problems, and now that comment can be included in future presentations.

I have video recorded some of my presentations as well. I'm an animated presenter, so a video recording captures all of the body language aspects of the presentation that the audio recording misses. If your stage is small, then you can set up the video camera on a tripod ahead of time and you are good to go. You don't need to have someone else get involved. If your stage is large, however, you really need to have someone shoot the video to keep you in the frame.

One downside to video recording that we should mention is that some companies, maybe even yours, will not want or authorize you to video record your presentation. If they do allow it, you need to let your audience know, and obtain permission, and that does tend to stifle the audience interaction because many folks become self-conscious. That obviously makes it harder to create a connection with them.

For these reasons, I like to video record my rehearsals (which we will discuss further in the next tool), and use my digital recorder for the actual presentation since it is so unobtrusive.

How do you incorporate the Review information that you now have? How do you make that next presentation better? That leads us to our next tool— Rehearsal.

REHEARSAL

As I type this section, I can't help but think of the presentation that I went to yesterday. I knew the presenter and prior to the presentation I asked, "Are you all prepared and ready to go?" He replied, "I didn't really have to prepare. I can wing it. I know what I have to say. I don't want to come across as phony or over-rehearsed."

Uh-oh. Have you ever had that feeling deep in your gut that you were about to witness a disaster—and there was nothing that you could do about it?

I'll spare you all the gory details, but in summary, the next 20 minutes were some of the most cringe-worthy presentation moments that I've ever witnessed, and I have seen my share of doozies. When I bumped into him later, after the presentation, he still had a shocked look on his face. "That was a disaster!" he said. "Everything that could go wrong—went wrong! Did I do anything right?" I racked my brain trying to come up with something positive to say—but unfortunately, nothing was jumping out at me. In desperation I finally blurted out, "Well, you remembered your name." He stared at me for a few seconds, and then we both burst out laughing. "It's not the end of the world," I said. "And, you did learn a valuable lesson—you learned that 'winging it' is not an effective strategy. Rehearsal has to be a regular part of your pre-presentation routine."

I stand by that advice. If you want to elevate your presentation to the next level, you have to get serious about using our next speaking tool—Rehearsal. Let's start with a clarification first. I'm talking about rehearsal, not practice. What? Isn't practice and rehearsal the same thing? Actually, no—they're different. One deals with working on specific skills, one deals with specific event preparation. Which is which? When you are working on a specific skill, you are practicing. For example, as mentioned in the delivery section, you might practice removing filler words from your speaking every time you open your mouth. Or, as mentioned in the Message section, you might practice creating a message using the 3 C's. In both of these examples you are working on improving a specific skill set that can help you in future presentations, so practice is definitely not a wasted effort.

When you are preparing for a specific event, in this case a specific presentation, the preparation that you are doing is best described with the word rehearsal. One of the reasons that I like the word rehearsal is that it has a connotation for most people of what actors do prior to a performance. I've never been an actor, but for years when I have given a presentation, I have felt the performance aspect was an important component of making it successful. Good actors and good presenters have a lot in common. Both are performing their craft before an audience. Both strive to create a connection with their audience. Both use their voice, their body language, and their words to get their message across. And finally, both aim to "be in the moment" while they are on the stage.

We do need to address the "I don't want to come across as phony or over-rehearsed" concern that my friend mentioned prior to his presentation. It's been my experience that the best presenters rehearse the most. That can't be a coincidence. I've had world-class presenters say that they have practiced their presentation 40-50-60+ times. I understand that some TED Talk speakers have rehearsed their 18-minute talks over 200 times. WOW! Your next question might be, "Why?" Why aren't they afraid of coming across phony or over-rehearsed? I believe the answer is counter-intuitive—the more you rehearse before a presentation, the less you focus on yourself during a presentation. This allows you to put more of your focus where it belongs, which is on your audience. Said a little simpler:

Having said all that, let's do a quick reality check. It's unlikely that most of you will have the time and opportunity to rehearse a presentation 200 times.

That DOESN'T mean that the alternative is no rehearsal at all, but it DOES mean that you need to be efficient with every rehearsal that you do conduct. So let's concentrate on ways that we can gain a good return on our investment in time with the following rehearsal rules:

- **REHEARSE OUT LOUD, NOT IN YOUR HEAD (PART 1)**

  Unless everyone in your audience is a mind reader, you will need to speak out loud to communicate with them. So why would you only rehearse your presentation in your head? If you have ever read aloud something that you have written, you quickly realize how differently we speak from how we write. An innocent sentence on a page can turn into a verbal tongue twister when we try to say it. You will only discover that if you rehearse out loud. This sounds so obvious, but you would be AMAZED how many presenters NEVER rehearse out loud. Don't be one of those folks! Oh, and don't do it in front of a mirror. I know that was advice you probably heard years ago, but the whole goal of rehearsing is to get to the point where you place less focus on yourself, which is hard to do if you are staring at yourself. I would rather you speak to your couch in your living room than the mirror.

- **REHEARSE OUT LOUD, NOT IN YOUR HEAD (PART 2)**

As you rehearse out loud, start mapping out where you will be standing on your stage as you give your presentation. In acting this is called "Blocking the Stage." Remember, you always want to move with purpose on the stage. For example, if you will be doing a Timeline, practice moving from section to section while you are speaking. Rehearsing your presentation with movement can be very helpful. For starters, it's easier to remember what you are supposed to be saying if there are specific spots on the stage where you say specific words, phrases, or stories. A second benefit is physical movement when rehearsing often helps facilitate retention of your material—it definitely works for me.

- **REHEARSE OUT LOUD, NOT IN YOUR HEAD (PART 3)**

At this point, after a few attempts, your rehearsals should start to flow better. It's time to quit talking to your couch and do a trial run with an actual audience. Although the ideal audience member would be someone who will be in your audience or is reflective of the knowledge, experience, and skill level that your audience will have, that's not always practical. This is where friends or family come in. I rehearse in front of my wife and son. I give them some background about the presentation and anything in particular that I want them to pay attention to. Rehearsing out loud, in front of an audience—even if the audience is only one or two people—will elevate your presentation performance so much higher than if you conduct all of your rehearsing in your head.

- **FOREST FOCUSED OR TREE FOCUSED**

Have you heard the phrase "Can't see the forest for the trees?" It means that sometimes we can get so focused on details (the trees) that we can miss the big picture (the forest). If I can modify this common phrase slightly, whether we are discussing a presentation or life in general, sometimes we need to be "forest focused" on the big picture, and sometimes we need to be "tree focused" on the details. For rehearsing a presentation we should be tree focused on the beginning and end of our presentation. Remember—we need to "Bang the Beginning" and have a "Killer Conclusion." So you should memorize these two sections because they are so critical. For the "forest focused" middle section of our presentation STRUCTURE (our M.E.A.N.S.) it is more important that you remember the meaning and the message behind the M.E.A.N.S. than knowing them word for word. As long as you are very clear on what you are trying to convey, the exact words are not as critical. So in summary: you don't need to memorize your entire presentation, just the beginning and ending. Make sense? If you try to memorize your entire presentation, it will put way too much pressure on yourself. Have you ever played a musical instrument? As a kid I played the accordion. (Stop laughing!) I was much better at memorizing music than sight-reading it. However, if I missed one (1) note, I was totally lost. I had to start over. Does this ring a bell with any of you? If you try to memorize your entire presentation, you can get too focused on what the next word is, and if you forget a word or phrase, then you are lost and you usually don't have an option to start a presentation over again. We want to move focus from yourself to your audience, right?

- **IT'S OKAY TO USE NOTES!**

There—I said it! It's okay to use notes to prompt you. But let me be clear—it's NOT okay to type out your entire presentation and read it to the audience. (This includes your Power Point slides, which we will discuss in further depth in a later section.) If you are reading this book, I can almost guarantee that you have attended a presentation that was read to you. How did you feel? Didn't it make you feel like you were back in Elementary School? Didn't you wonder why you even needed to be attending the presentation since you could have read the information to yourself at your own desk? I won't beat this to death—just remember that Notes = okay. Reading entire presentation to audience = NOT okay.

Notes should be in bullet point format, with no more than a sentence for each bullet point. A word or two is best. They're there just to jump start your memory if you lose your place. There are various opinions on whether these notes should be on 3X5 cards, or on a single page of paper if possible, etc. I don't have strong feelings on this, so do what matches your style or the situation. However, I will relay that I once had some notes for a presentation on 3X5 cards, and I managed to drop the cards and get them all out of order because I hadn't numbered them. Grrrrrrrr! Learn from my mistake—if your notes are on more than one card or piece of paper, be sure to number them!

- **RECORD YOUR REHEARSAL**

This is such a valuable tool! As I mentioned earlier, I really like to video record my rehearsals. If the recording is not too long, it allows me the chance to play it back in a particular way that might be considered unusual. The first time I play it back, I watch it with the sound off. That helps me focus on my body language. If you have an odd gesture or physical mannerism that is distracting, it will be very obvious very quickly. I also look to see if I'm moving with purpose or just pacing the stage. Next, I play it back with only the sound, no picture. I can focus now on my voice and my words. Am I projecting my voice well? Am I rushing? Am I using too many filler words? How are my transitions between my points? Is my message clear? Lastly, I watch the recording with the picture and the sound together. I imagine that I'm watching someone else at a Toastmasters meeting, and I'm their evaluator. How would I critique what I just saw? What were the strong points and what needed work? By imagining I'm critiquing someone else rather than myself, I think it helps me be more neutral and less emotional with my self-assessment. If the presentation is longer, or I'm under a time constraint, I won't watch each of my recordings in this manner, but I always try to watch at least one recording this way.

- **REHEARSE ANY PLANNED EXERCISES/ACTIVITIES**

  If you recall from the CONTENT tool section, I mentioned that to avoid chaos, you need to be extremely clear with your instructions on what you want them to do, and you also need to have a way set up ahead of time to regain their attention when you are ready to move on. If you have a small rehearsal audience of family or friends, it will enable you to determine if the instructions that YOU think are extremely clear are equally clear to your audience. It's much easier to make a correction in rehearsal than it is during the actual presentation!

- **REHEARSE USING YOUR EQUIPMENT AND PROPS**

  If you are using a projector, make sure that you know how to set up and operate it. If you will be using a Power Point remote control, make sure you know how to work it. If you are using props, be sure to include using them in your rehearsal. For a Toastmasters contest speech, I had a prop that included Styrofoam cups, strings, and paperclips. Without boring you with all of the details, I needed to have one of the cups end up on the floor. How hard could that be? Well, with this particular prop, it was easier said than done. I had to rehearse this dozens of times until I learned how to do it correctly. The prop would have failed miserably during that speech without that rehearsal—I wouldn't have even known it was that difficult if I hadn't given it a try ahead of time.

- **REHEARSE ON YOUR ACTUAL STAGE IF POSSIBLE**

  If you can, conduct a "dress rehearsal" on the actual stage that you will be giving the presentation on. This will give you a chance to iron out any kinks in your presentation, and it will definitely improve your effectiveness on "game day." The night before a Toastmasters District Contest speech, while the room was still being prepared, I was able to talk my way past the front desk and rehearse my speech a couple of times on the actual stage. It gave me a shot of confidence that definitely helped the next day. There was an ironic moment the next day, though. When I entered the large conference room I was surprised to see that the stage had been moved from where it was just a few hours earlier! It was still the same room, however, and when I gave my speech, I felt so much more comfortable having been on that stage in that room beforehand, even if it was in a different location.

- **"GO BIG OR GO HOME"**

Are you familiar with that phrase? In this context it means to do your rehearsal "all out"—don't just go through the motions. In fact, during rehearsal, exaggeration is your friend. If you know that you typically need to speak louder, speak WAY louder. If you know that you typically need to speak slower, speak WAY slower. By going all out and even exaggerating during your rehearsal, it helps you find that "sweet spot" during your actual presentation. If it helps, think of the baseball player who is on deck, waiting for their turn to bat. Often you will see them swinging a bat with a donut-shaped weight on it to make the bat heavier during their warm-up. When it is their turn to come to the plate, they take the weight off so the bat feels lighter to them when they swing. By exaggerating all aspects of your delivery performance during rehearsal, your actual presentation can feel "lighter" and more relaxed and in that sweet spot.

I want to add a quick thought regarding another benefit of Rehearsal—Time Management. Most presentations do not have an "open ended" time frame—there is usually a set amount of time that you have to fit your presentation into. If you know that you have a 15 minute time slot, and your rehearsals are consistently going over that, then you know you have to trim some time from somewhere in the presentation. Better to do that trimming in Rehearsal than having to do it on the fly DURING the presentation. If despite your best efforts you are still over your time frame, you can check with the appropriate person and see if your time can be extended. I had a friend who liked to say, "You can't put 10 pounds of cement in a 5 pound bag." In your presentation, don't try to cram 10 pounds of information into a 5-pound time-frame bag. It's a disservice to your audience and creates more stress for you. It's better to deliver less material well than more material less well.

Using the Rehearsal tool effectively will definitely separate you from most presenters, and will allow you to elevate your presentations to the next level. Our last Presentation Elevation tool, RESOURCES, will also help you continue your journey to becoming an AWESOME PRESENTER!

RESOURCES

I remember a teacher in high school once telling me, "You can put a lot of effort in doing something, but if you are heading east looking for the sunset, than all that effort is wasted. You need to put your effort in the right direction to have a chance of success." Although the name of the teacher has slipped my memory, that message never has. We are bombarded with information on a daily basis, and often it's not clear what information—or resources—are helpful and what are not. For our last Presentation Elevation tool, RESOURCES, I'll steer you towards the organizations, people, books, and programs that I have found to be particularly valuable in my own journey—and I believe that you will find them useful as well.

TOASTMASTERS INTERNATIONAL

I've mentioned Toastmasters several times in this book so far. I currently belong to three clubs, including an advanced club, and being a member has been tremendously helpful in my quest to improve my presentation skills. For those of you not familiar with the organization, it was founded in 1924 by Ralph C. Smedley, who saw a need to provide people with an opportunity to improve their public speaking skills. Toastmasters International is a worldwide nonprofit educational organization whose mission states, "We empower individuals to become more effective communicators and leaders." Per a Toastmasters International August 5, 2015 news release, there are now 332,000 members in 15,400 clubs in 135 countries. Toastmasters' website is:

www.toastmasters.org

Okay, okay, that's all the background, but why should you care? Because Toastmasters provides a non-intimidating, supportive, and fun environment to work on your public speaking, presentation, and leadership skills. (Note—The following is based on my experience with one or more of the clubs I belong to—your experience at your local club may vary.)

Most clubs have two separate sections of their meetings—one section is where people get to do impromptu talks for 1-2 minutes. (Toastmasters call this section "Table Topics.") The second section is where 1-3 people deliver prepared speeches, usually between 5-7 minutes. There are several functionaries that you may see at a typical meeting. A Toastmaster runs the meeting. A Table Topics Master coordinates the impromptu speaking section of the meeting. A General Evaluator evaluates the Table Topic speakers and the meeting as a whole. Each Speaker has a specific Evaluator to evaluate their speech and give a 2-3 minute report to the group. A Grammarian reviews excellent and not so excellent grammar usage and vocabulary. An "Ah" Counter identifies crutch and filler words that speakers are using. Finally, a Timer monitors the time of all of the speakers.

The more you stand up and speak before an audience, the more comfortable you get and the better you become. There are several manuals with many "speaking projects" that focus on a particular skill that will help you improve your ability. I've found the skills you learn by doing the functionary roles to be equally valuable.

Many companies sponsor a Toastmasters club on site or at a nearby location. If you're not sure, it's definitely worthwhile to check with your Human Resources or Training and Development Department.

In addition to all of the above, many Toastmasters clubs also have various speaking contests during the year, including a Table Topics contest, a Humorous Speech contest, and an Evaluation contest. For these contests, the winner of a Club contest will next move to an Area contest, which is made up of several clubs. The winner of the Area contest next competes at the Division contest, which is made up of several Areas. Lastly, the winner of the Division contest competes with other Division winners at the District contest, which is made up of several Divisions. At the District contest 1st, 2nd, and 3rd places are awarded.

The one contest that is different is the International Speech Contest. This is a worldwide contest. It follows the same format as the other contests, except that the winner of the District contest moves on to the Semi-Finals. There are nine Semi-Finalist brackets, and the winner of each bracket moves to the Finals. One of those nine Finalists becomes the World Champion of Public Speaking for that year—the best of the best. Interestingly enough, for the Finals the speakers have to give a different speech than the one that they used in the other rounds of this competition. To reach the Semi-Finals of this competition, you have to be a very good speaker. To reach the Finals, you have to be a great speaker. To win and become the World Champion—you have established yourself as an extraordinary speaker. I've been lucky enough to meet and learn from people who have made it to this upper echelon, and I consider them valuable resources to elevate your presentations to the next level. Let's meet some of them:

CRAIG VALENTINE

Craig Valentine is the 1999 World Champion of Public Speaking. His website is www.craigvalentine.com. He has a lot of information available on his site, and I recommend that you check it out.

Craig is the co-author of the book *World Class Speaking*. I really enjoyed this book. It is divided into three sections, with the second and third sections devoted to marketing a professional speaking business, which is not the goal of most of you reading my book. However, the first section is on mastering the art of public speaking and is very educational and entertaining.

Craig is also one of the authors of the follow-up book, *World Class Speaking in Action*. In this book, 50 individuals who trained with Craig and became Certified World Class Speaking Coaches each contributed a chapter to this book. As in the first book, there are chapters geared more to the professional speaker, but there are also many chapters on all aspects of creating effective presentations with helpful tips and tricks.

One area where Craig is a master is in the art of storytelling. When you are ready to take your storytelling to a much higher level, you might want to check out his EDGE OF THEIR SEATS STORYTELLING—HOME STUDY COURSE FOR SPEAKERS! I've utilized several of his techniques in my presentations from this course with great success.

DARREN LACROIX

Darren LaCroix is the 2001 World Champion of Public Speaking. His website is www.darrenlacroix.com. Like Craig Valentine, he also has a tremendous amount of information available on that site—including blogs and video lessons—in addition to the many products that he has created over the years. Darren is one of the reasons that I decided to join Toastmasters. I saw his championship speech on YouTube several years ago, and it was so great, it made me want to learn more about him and Toastmasters. His speech was one of the best-crafted speeches I have ever seen—I definitely recommend checking it out.

While you are on YouTube, you should know that Darren has many videos regarding all aspects of public speaking and presentation skills. Most of the videos are between 2-5 minutes, and they are well worth your time.

As a former stand-up comedian, Darren is an expert at developing and utilizing humor in presentations. I attended his Humor Champ Camp that he taught along with Tim Gard (who we will also be discussing in this section) and after two days, I came away with many ideas of how to incorporate humor in my speaking. This topic is so important that I'll be discussing it further in the BONUS section of this book, along with two specific products of Darren's— *Improv to Improve!*—and *Humor 101*.

ED TATE

Ed Tate is the 2000 World Champion of Public Speaking. To learn more about Ed, you can visit his website at www.edtate.com. Ed is a tremendous trainer and facilitator. I've been able to watch several of his live keynote presentations and breakout sessions and I am in awe of his skill level at getting his audience fully engaged.

TIM GARD

Tim Gard is a Certified Speaking Professional (CSP), which is a designation established by the National Speakers Association (NSA). Tim is also a member of NSA's Speaker Hall of Fame as a result of receiving a Council of Peers Award for Excellence (CPAE). Tim's website is at www.timgard.com.

What these designations basically mean is that Tim has performed as a professional speaker at the highest level for many years. Along with Darren LaCroix, Tim is also an expert at developing and utilizing humor in presentations, which is why they were such a great team for the Humor Champ Camp that I attended in 2014. Tim is especially effective with his use of props during his speaking. I've had the pleasure of seeing Tim in person several times, and I just love how he integrates his humor, his props, and his points so seamlessly. You can see him in action by either checking out the videos on his website, or the Tim Gard Whoo Hoo Channel on YouTube—link below: www.youtube.com/user/TimGardWooHoo/featured. Tim is also on Twitter:

https://twitter.com/funwithtim

PATRICIA FRIPP

Like Tim Gard, Patricia Fripp is also a CSP and Hall of Fame Speaker. She is a past president, and first female president, of the NSA. She has also received NSA's most prestigious speaking honor, the Cavett Award, which is considered the "Oscar" of the speaking world. Patricia's website is at www.fripp.com. In addition to her various products, be sure to check out the free resources that she has available. You should also check out Patricia's highly interactive, learn-at-your-own-pace, online training at www.frippVT.com.

Many professional presenters consider Patricia the best speaking coach in the United States. I've watched Patricia coach speakers "live" on stage numerous times at speaking conferences, and am amazed at her ability to improve a speech. I've quoted her a few times in this book because I find her insight so valuable and top-notch.

MANLEY FEINBERG

Manley Feinberg is one of those individuals who has skills in multiple areas. He is a professional speaker, an author of one of the chapters in the book *World Class Speaking in Action*, a professional musician, and a noted photographer. To top it off he has a speaking voice I would kill for. It really doesn't seem fair—I'm not sure there is anything he can't do. Manley's website is at www.verticallessons.com.

In the Bonus section of this book, we are going to discuss how to more effectively use PowerPoint in your presentations. I will be referencing some of Manley's comments and suggestions, as I have found them to be extremely helpful and useful. His web address for his information on PowerPoint is at www.verticallessons.com/World-Class-PowerPointOI.

MAUREEN MERRILL

Maureen Merrill is great! Maureen's business, Maureen Merrill Consulting, is based in northern California, and provides highly professional, personalized coaching. Maureen's graduate degree in psychology and many years' experience as an entrepreneur and community leader inspire her passion for a world that communicates brilliantly. She facilitates retreats for boards and teams, and provides workshops and "boot camps" in public speaking and customer service. I've been lucky enough to attend some of these "boot camps" and found them to be practical, fun, and full of insight. Maureen is an expert in social confidence and personal presence, and she can help any person or organization communicate more effectively and persuasively. Her website is at www.maureenmerrill.com.

TED TALKS

TED stands for Technology, Entertainment, and Design. TED's tagline is "Ideas worth spreading."

Some of the brightest and most thought-provoking individuals in the world outline their "big ideas" in presentations that can be no longer than 18 minutes. You can check out some of the greatest presentations ever given at www.ted.com, or on YouTube. One delivery technique that most of the presenters use is to make their presentation very conversational, like they are speaking directly to you, and it makes these talks very effective. I highly recommend checking them out.

Talk Like TED by Carmine Gallo

Once you have the chance to watch some TED talks—and I'm sure that they'll impress you—you might wonder, "What made that talk so good?" This book describes the "secret sauce" used by the best TED presenters in their talks, and it is as impressive as the TED talks themselves. Great book!

11 Deadly Presentation Sins by Rob Biesenbach

If you want to deliver a successful presentation, then you need to avoid these "Sins." Rob is a corporate communications expert, a public speaker, and also an actor, and this book is written from all three perspectives. He included a specific concept from digital marketing expert and professional speaker

Mitch Joel that completely changed my perspective on PowerPoint, and we'll discuss it in the Bonus section.

Taking Flight! by Merrick Rosenberg & Daniel Silvert

This book takes the DISC Behavioral Styles that I mentioned in the AUDIENCE section (and elaborated on in the BONUS section) and brings them to life by using an entertaining fable to illustrate the interactions of all four styles. The fable format is unique and makes the book easy to read and easy to understand—I really enjoyed it. I have also attended two TAKING FLIGHT WITH DISC training sessions based on the book, and all participants in my two sessions gave the training very high marks.

Note: As I'm editing this, Merrick has just come out with a new book, called *The Chameleon*, which includes 22 fables about the personality styles. You can check out an animated book trailer that describes the book at: http://bit.ly/TheChameleon-Trailer.

CREATIVELIVE—Heroic Public Speaking

CREATIVELIVE is a site that offers online classes on many topics. Their website is www.creativelive.com. One of the classes that they offer is called Heroic Public Speaking. The instructors for this class are Michael and Amy Port. Both of them are professional actors and speaking coaches, and in this course they teach how to create a presentation that is more like a performance. Michael is also a bestselling author, and at the time of writing this section, I just finished reading his latest book, *Steal the Show*, where Michael explains how to make the most of every presentation and interaction that you have.

Let's do a recap of our PRESENTATION ELEVATION tools before we move on to the BONUS section.

REVIEW

Feedback DURING the presentation

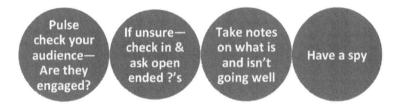

Feedback AFTER the presentation

Reviewing the feedback

- Two types—"Impact" and "Style"
- "Impact" takes priority over "Style"
- When reviewing feedback think "Buffet"
- The best evaluators also use feedback the best

Recording the presentation

- "Record your speech and it will teach"
- Digital audio recorders are a great tool
- Review for "gems" and "germs"
- Video is great if practical and allowed

REHEARSAL

- Rehearsal is different than practice.

- Rehearse out loud—not in your head.

- Know when to be forest focused and when to be tree focused.

- It's ok to use notes.

- Record your rehearsal.

- Rehearse any planned exercises/activities.

- Rehearse using your equipment and props.

- Rehearse on your actual stage if possible.

- "Go big or go home"

RESOURCES

Organizations—Toastmasters International, TED

People—Craig Valentine, Darren LaCroix, Ed Tate, Tim Gard, Patricia Fripp, Manley Feinberg, Maureen Merrill, Michael Port

Books—*World Class Speaking, World Class Speaking In Action, Talk Like TED, 11 Deadly Presentation Sins, Taking Flight, The Chameleon,* and *Steal the Show*

Programs—EDGE OF THEIR SEATS STORYTELLING: HOME STUDY COURSE FOR SPEAKERS, IMPROV TO IMPROVE!, HUMOR 101, HEROIC PUBLIC SPEAKING

Bonus Section

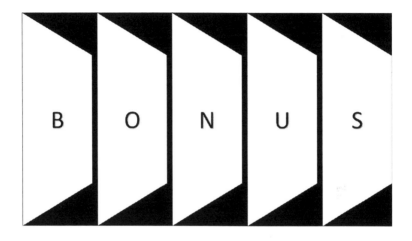

Isn't it great when you receive a bonus? I think so too. I had some miscellaneous tips on several topics that I wanted to share. Let's dive right in!

POWERPOINT

I've heard Manley Feinberg say that more than 30 million PowerPoint presentations are estimated to be delivered every day. Holy smokes—that's a big number! I wonder how many of those 30 million were effective? From personal experience, I'm guessing the answer is "not many."

At a recent presentation I was giving, I happened to mention that I wouldn't be using PowerPoint—and the audience applauded! Why? I believe it is because presenters forget that PowerPoint is a visual aid, not the presentation itself. So if PowerPoint is a visual aid, how do we use that visual aid more effectively?

Let's start by making this visual aid as visual as we can—we can do that by reducing the amount of words and bullet points we use on the slide. Manley suggests the "5 Alive" rule—no more than 5 bullet points per slide, and no more than 5 words per bullet point. Again, that should be the max—the fewer (or no) bullet points used, the better. One easy way to ensure that you are not using too many words on each slide is to use a bigger font. This has the added benefit of making what words you do have much more readable. Ever try to read a 12-point, or smaller, font on the projection screen? It's maddening, isn't it?

There is another advantage of using fewer words/bigger font on your slides—it keeps the presenter from reading the entire presentation to their audience. As I mentioned in the REHEARSAL section, it's okay to use notes, but most audiences hate to have a presentation read to them. I know I do.

Many poor presenters like to "Data Dump" tons of data, stats, and numbers on their PowerPoint slides. Manley says, "The meaning of the data is more important than all the data." I've also heard him say, "If a picture is worth a thousand words, it's worth a million numbers."

Tagging on to Manley's comments, do you have to use any words at all? As Rob Biesenbach mentioned in his book, *11 Deadly Presentation Sins*, he had a colleague who liked to say, "'Insert text here' is a suggestion, not a command." Studies have shown that visuals are up to six times more effective for memory retention than words alone are.

Where can you get visuals to replace the verbiage? First, check to see if your company has a "visual image library" or a stock photography contract with a catalog of images that you can access. Another option is to use your own pictures. The main point is, don't just yank an image off the Internet that belongs to someone else—that's not okay. In Manley's *World Class Speaking in Action* chapter (Chapter 24), he provides additional suggestions on how to make these visuals work for you.

I have a few pet peeves regarding PowerPoint. One of them is when a presenter leaves the slide up on the screen even though the presentation has moved on to another item or topic. I find it very distracting, and I think most audiences do as well. To avoid this as a presenter, think "PowerPoint Wannabe." Why? Because you "want to hit that B key often!" On most laptops and computer keyboards, if you hit the "B" key during a PowerPoint presentation, it blanks the screen. It takes the audience's focus from the screen and puts it back on you as the presenter. Most wireless presentation remote controls also have a button that will blank the screen. Don't be afraid to use it!

There's an even better way to be a "PowerPoint Wannabe"—you can include a "B" slide in your presentation. In this case the "B" stands for Black. Why is this option even better? When you use the "B" key to blank the screen, hitting the "B" key again brings you back to the slide you were originally on. If your presentation has moved on from that slide, it can be a little confusing to your audience. However, if you have a black slide inserted into the PowerPoint presentation when you want the focus back on you, when you are ready to move on you can advance to the next slide seamlessly, either from the computer keyboard or your presentation remote. Whichever "PowerPoint Wannabe" option you choose will put you miles ahead of most presenters.

I would like to leave the topic of PowerPoint with a final thought that I learned from Rob Biesenbach's book *11 Deadly Presentation Sins*. Rob mentions the thoughts of professional speaker Mitch Joel that some of the most effective PowerPoint slides should mean nothing to someone who didn't attend your presentation. WOW! That was definitely a novel concept and a real "Aha" moment for me. If you have that mindset, then PowerPoint automatically returns to being a visual aid—a tool to enhance your presentation—not the presentation itself.

HUMOR

Why should we include humor in a presentation? Basically, more humor makes it more fun, and when people are having more fun the presentation is more memorable, so their retention is a lot higher. Said another way: it enhances learning.

If you are in agreement that humor should be a part of our presentations, what do I mean by "humor?" Humor is easy to recognize, but a little more difficult to define, and everyone's definition is a little different. Humor typically includes such things as misdirection, something unexpected, exaggeration, pattern interrupt, combining things that don't go together, etc.

So, should you go up and just tell a bunch of jokes? Definitely not! You're a presenter, not a stand-up comedian. The goals are different. The stand-up wants to get as many laughs as they can during their set. As a presenter, you have a message that you want to convey, and the humor is just another tool to help convey that message to the audience. There should always be a point to your presentation humor.

Well, how do we add humor then? I've heard Craig Valentine say on many occasions, "Never add humor to a speech, uncover it." What Craig is saying is to not try to force humor into your presentation. Have you ever sat through a presentation when the humor seemed to be forced and didn't really support the message? The humor might even have been funny, but didn't it leave you with a "that didn't really have anything to do with the presentation" feeling?

If we don't want to add it, how do we "uncover it?" One of the easiest ways is in the dialogue of the characters in our stories. As we discussed in the delivery section, when you tell a story, you need a mix of narration and dialogue. You can't have just one or the other. Typically, beginning presenters use too much narration. Dialogue should not only drive the story to your message, it should also drive the humor too. Just as an example, in the introduction, I relayed a story of my first and worst presentation ever. I've used this story as my intro to some of my Effective Presentation classes. If you recall, the story's climax is when one young lady in the front row turned to the young lady next to her and said—in a loud stage whisper—"He's really nervous, isn't he?" When I tell this story, it accomplishes several positive things. First, it definitely takes me off of any pedestal my audience might have initially put me on—it makes me more relatable and just "real." It makes the audience want to avoid the PAIN (remember the 3 P's?) of what happened to me, which gives them an incentive to learn about the tools for effective presentations. And let's face it, since it's not happening to them, it's funny. Self-deprecating humor works well to show that you don't take yourself too seriously, and it gives the audience permission to have a laugh at your expense.

I even had some humor in the first two lines in my first/worst presentation story set-up. "Have you ever attended a bad presentation?" While I say the line, I'm smiling and raising my hand. The audience smiles and raises their hands also, because pretty much everybody has attended a bad presentation. Then when I ask the follow-up question, "Was it YOUR presentation?" I get a lot of sheepish looks, smiles, raised hands to match my raised hand, and usually some laughs.

I grant you, none of this results in gut-busting laughter, but it is humorous, it lightens the mood, and it indicates right off the bat that we—presenter and audience—are going to have some fun.

Some humor tips that I learned in the Humor Champ Camp instructed by Darren LaCroix and Tim Gard are as follows:

- When it comes to your humor content, when in doubt—leave it out. You never want to offend or insult anyone in your audience.

- Put the punch word or words at the end of the sentence. For example, Henny Youngman's famous line was, "Take my wife—PLEASE!" It wouldn't have worked if he said, "PLEASE take my wife!"

- The shorter the setup, the more "punch" the punch word or words have. Don't meander around with your setup.

- We have already discussed the "Rule of 3" in our structure section. This rule is used extensively in the world of comedy. Usually the first two examples are logical, and the third is unexpected or an exaggeration. "To be an effective presenter you need CLARITY, SINCERITY, and VALIUM." (Okay, okay—I won't quit my day job!)

As I mentioned earlier, I also learned how effective props can be. Tim Gard is a master of using props to give added meaning to his message and his points. (He even sells some of the props that he uses in his presentations on his web site.) Props get your audience involved, and can help make your message more memorable. They can be small like something you can keep in your pocket (pocket props) or bigger and more elaborate. They don't always have to be humorous, but they should always support your takeaway message. For example, I once used a prop of a wooden figure holding a box as part of a safety demonstration on safe lifting. It's difficult to describe the prop, but the point is that everyone loved the visual, and it helped make the presentation a lot more fun. I know for a fact that it also made the presentation memorable, because years later I had some of those audience members ask me to bring "Lift-ee" (what I named him) back for a repeat performance!

The last takeaway I want to share from the Humor Champ Camp is to try to look for the humor in every situation. Those events that you will laugh about later? Why not laugh about them now? Things will go wrong as a presenter: electricity will go out, unexpected earthquake drill, projector won't work, etc. (I've had all of these things, and more, happen to me.) As I've heard Ed Tate say, "People who speak don't have bad days, they just have new material!" Try to keep a "humor mindset," and it will serve both you and your audience well.

How can you improve including humor in your presentation? If you want to "flex that humor muscle," as Tim Gard says, how can you exercise it? I've already put in a plug for Toastmasters, but I'm going to do it again. As I've already mentioned, there is a section in most Toastmasters meetings where members get a chance to give impromptu speeches— "Table Topics." This is an excellent way to practice "thinking on your feet," which is a great skill to master as a presenter. Unexpected events are going to occur during most presentations, and if you keep that "humor mindset" and develop the ability to think on your feet, you can make those unexpected events work in your favor.

Another way to "flex that humor muscle" is to take an Improv class. I've attended a keynote presentation by Darren LaCroix where he had the audience participate in several improv exercises. It was great! His DVD product, IMPROV TO IMPROVE, was actually video recorded at that same presentation. (It was a little surreal seeing myself in a couple of the audience shots!) Attending that keynote really opened my eyes to how valuable improv can be to help you be "in the moment" when you are on stage—and being "in the moment" is a crucial skill to create a connection with your audience.

Lastly, as Darren likes to say, "Funny people think differently." There is a structure and a process to creating humor that can help, even if you don't think you are funny. Darren's HUMOR 101 DVD dives into some of the structure and process that Darren followed to improve. He even supplies proof—you get to see video from his disastrous first time on the comedy stage, and his transformation from that disaster to the speech he gave that won him the title of World Champion of Public Speaking in 2001. I found his journey to be incredibly inspirational. I think you will too.

AUDIENCE BEHAVIORAL STYLES

I mentioned in the Audience section that a helpful way to research/profile your future audience is by utilizing a Behavioral Style analysis, such as the DISC method. Many of you probably have some familiarity with DISC, but for those of you who don't, it is a theory on human behavior that was developed in the 1920's by psychologist William Marston. Each letter in DISC stood for a different behavioral style. The D stood for Dominance, the I stood for Influence, the S stood for Steadiness, and the C stood for Conscientiousness. Over the years there have been several variations of this "4 Box" DISC model that have been created. There are many companies that offer different types of DISC assessment testing that you can take if you want to know what behavioral style you are.

Having participated in several different DISC assessments over the years, I've found all of them useful for helping to understand folks that I was interacting with. For this book, I created my own "down and dirty" DISC-inspired behavioral analysis. Before we get to my chart, I want to make clear that there is no behavioral style that is "best" or "worst." Whether we are talking about a company's employees or society in general, all four styles are needed and are valuable.

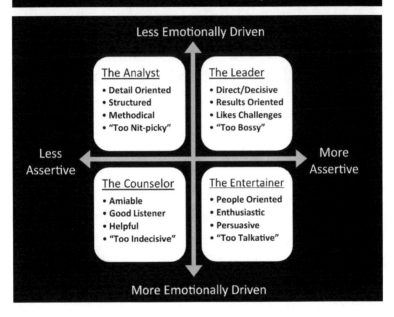

Let's analyze my chart. You will notice that there are two dimensions (represented by the two arrows) that influence the four main behavioral styles. Those two dimensions are Assertiveness and Emotionally Driven. People tend to have more or less of these two dimensions. People who exhibit more assertive behavior fall into the boxes on the right, less assertive behavior fall into the boxes on the left. The boxes at the bottom are for folks whose behavior is more emotionally driven, and the boxes at the top reflect less emotionally driven behavior.

Very few people are solely one style—most of us are a combination. Different settings can influence this too. Do you know anyone whose behavior at home is completely different than during work hours? Am I describing you? Having said all that, in a particular setting, there is usually one style that tends to dominate our behavior. Let's discuss each of the four behavioral styles and see if we can identify which one best describes you.

THE ANALYST—As you can see from the dimensional arrows, these people are less assertive and less emotionally driven. They are often described as "detail oriented" and accuracy is very important to them. They are more comfortable with facts than feelings. They like to be organized, which is why they prefer a structured environment. They are precise in their language and methodical in their approach. They are usually very punctual. If this behavior is taken to an extreme, it could be labeled as "too nitpicky." I named this style THE ANALYST, and other occupations or departments where these folks tend to gravitate to would include auditors, accountants, and engineers. Famous folks who fit this style would include Bill Gates and Albert Einstein.

THE LEADER—The dimensional arrows on this style indicate that these people are more assertive and less emotionally driven. They like to be direct and to the point. These are often described as "take charge individuals" with a bias towards action. They are definitely results oriented. They enjoy a challenge, and love the feeling of accomplishment. They work at a fast pace and are disciplined about time. If this behavior is taken to an extreme, it could be labeled as "too bossy." I named this style THE LEADER because you will find many people in Senior Leadership positions in the workplace that fit this profile. Well-known individuals who fall into this category would include Donald Trump and Ted Turner.

THE COUNSELOR—The dimensional arrows reflect that this style is less assertive and more emotionally driven. These folks are good listeners, friendly, helpful, and loyal. They like working cooperatively with others. Being more emotionally driven, feelings factor strongly in their decision making process. They are often described as "steady" or "easy going" individuals who try to avoid conflict. They work at a slower pace and are flexible regarding time. If this behavior is taken to an extreme, it could be labeled as "too indecisive." I named this style THE COUNSELOR because you will typically find counselors, therapists, and HR personnel who fit this profile. Famous examples would include Charlie Brown and Mr. Rogers.

THE ENTERTAINER—Last, but certainly not least, this behavioral style includes individuals who are more assertive and more emotionally driven. They are people oriented and enthusiastic. They love to talk, and because they are effective communicators, they can use that verbal ability to be very persuasive. They are often described as "lively," or the "life of the party," which makes sense since they do love an audience. They think fast, talk fast, and act fast. They are passionate in what they are doing, and tend to lose all track of time. If this behavior is taken to an extreme, it could be labeled as "too talkative." I named this style THE ENTERTAINER because you will find these outgoing and extroverted people gravitate towards positions in sales and marketing and other public relations type work. Well-known examples would include the late Robin Williams and Oprah Winfrey.

Now that we have described the four behavioral styles, which one of them best describes you? As I stated earlier, most people have some characteristics from each style, but there is usually one style that you revert to under pressure. If you still are not sure, ask a close friend or co-worker or family member—it's sometimes easier to recognize these traits in others than in ourselves.

While writing this chapter, I had a funny situation come up which is a perfect example of these behavioral styles in action. I was going to a lunch meeting with folks from all four of the behavioral style categories. THE COUNSELORS wanted to know what everyone was ordering. "What are you having?" "That sounds great—I think I'll have that." "Oh, what are you having? That sounds great too. Now I'm not sure what to have. What do you think I should have?" I think they all might still be at the restaurant deciding. When the bill came due, THE ANALYSTS huddled together and, after checking and double-checking their calculations, announced that everyone owed $16.32 for their share. Once the meal was over, THE LEADERS disappeared as they had places to go and things to do—no time for chitchat. In contrast, during the entire meal, dessert, and even out into the parking lot, THE ENTERTAINERS were telling animated stories to their captive audience.

One other item to be aware of is that we tend to have the most difficulty dealing with the behavioral style that is diagonally across from our style on the chart. Typically the ANALYSTS and ENTERTAINERS and the LEADERS and COUNSELORS have more challenges relating to each other. Based on the chart and the descriptions, can you see how that can happen? However, any style that is different from yours can be challenging.

Why does this matter? I'll use a personal one-on-one example to illustrate how this works. My current boss joined our organization about two years ago. In one of our early interactions he told me, "Don, when I want to know what time it is, I don't need you to build me a watch." Ouch—that hurt a little bit. Before asking you to guess what behavioral styles we both are, I'll give you a couple of additional pieces of information. My boss is a retired military veteran who is a stickler for being on time and likes to get to the point in a conversation. On the other hand, I like to tell a story during my conversations, the more interesting and exciting, the happier I am. What is my style, and what is my boss's style? Check the chart and the above descriptions to assist you in making that determination.

Welcome back. If you guessed that my boss is THE LEADER, you would be correct. If you guessed that I was THE ENTERTAINER, you would also be correct. What my boss was trying to tell me with his watch analogy is that if he wants a specific piece of information, I should just give it to him without the "frills." I now try to give him the executive summary of a situation up front, and only if he requests it do I give him all the nitty-gritty details. I've adapted my communication approach to better fit with his style.

My boss has also adapted his approach to match my style. Since I'm in THE ENTERTAINER category, I'm a people person who is more emotionally driven than my boss. He will now often start a conversation asking how I'm doing and how I'm feeling before diving in to what he wants to discuss.

The reason all of this matters is because knowing your behavioral style and the primary style of your audience can help you modify your approach to your presentation and build a better connection with that audience.

Now you might be thinking, "What if I'm unable to determine the primary behavioral style of my audience, or what if all four styles are represented in my audience? What do I do then?"

Good questions! You can still utilize this information to modify your approach to the presentation. I recommend the following four steps—taken in order:

1. For THE LEADER—give the "forest focused"/"mile-high" view right off the bat—cut to the chase/get to the point.

2. For THE ENTERTAINER—tap their enthusiasm. They can be persuasive toward others, so you want to bring that positive energy front and center.

3. For THE COUNSELOR—address the emotional component. There is almost always a "human element" in a situation—so spotlight what that element is.

4. For THE ANALYST—these folks have been waiting patiently for the "tree-focused" details—the step by step on what needs to be done.

Using these four steps will allow you to "tweak" the effective presentation tools that you have learned throughout this book. I have found it particularly useful for the "Killer Conclusion" at the end of a presentation where I indicate "Next Steps" that I would like the audience to take. An extra bonus tip— using these four steps when you are sending an informational email to a large mixed behavioral style group will definitely make that email more effective— give it a try.

MISCELLANEOUS BONUS PRESENTATION TIPS AND TRICKS

When you are soliciting comments from your audience, when you want more, say "What else?" It generates more conversation. When you want to stop the comments and move on, say "Anything else?" It ends the conversation. I've used "What else?" and "Anything else?" many times—and it really works!

When you gesture towards your audience—don't point. Pointing turns people off. It reminds people of being lectured to when they were a kid. Some audience members find it threatening. A better way is to use a palm up/open hand gesture, which eliminates all of the negative connotations that pointing has. Give it a try in your next presentation.

Chaim Eyal had some great tips that he allowed me to share with you:

- Three Don'ts: 1. Don't ever apologize. 2. Don't ever admit to being nervous. 3. Don't ever admit mistakes—unless you offend someone. If that happens, apologize and move on.

- If you lose your place in your presentation, you can ask your audience for help. (Chaim called this the Colombo method—you younger folks will have to Google that reference!)

- I mentioned this earlier but it's worth repeating: When you look up, it means, "I'm thinking." When you look down, it means, "I'm lost." (Of course, it's always best to maintain eye contact with your audience, but if you do look away, looking up is better than looking down!)

Chaim also discussed with me the importance of having a back- up plan in case there are Stage issues that occur—specifically if your "technology" for the presentation is not available. He relayed a story of one two-hour presentation that was interrupted after fifteen minutes by a fire alarm. Everyone was evacuated to the front lawn. Twenty minutes later, an announcement was made that no one would be able to return to the building for at least another 90 minutes. Chaim delivered the rest of the presentation on the lawn, in the shade of a tree, without any audio-visual at all. He told me that it was one of his best presentations. Wow—talk about turning lemons into lemonade!

Chaim was able to turn this unexpected situation around because he routinely prepared himself for the possibility that everything that can go wrong in a presentation—will, at some point. Do YOU have a back-up plan in case your technology is not being "cooperative" or is unavailable? Could you use handouts, or a flip chart, or include some additional exercises? Think about it. So the final tip for our BONUS Section is as follows:

- Have a "no technology available" back-up plan for your presentation. At some point, you will need to use it.

Final Thoughts

TAKING *"PRESENTATION ROAD"* FROM AWFUL TO AWESOME!

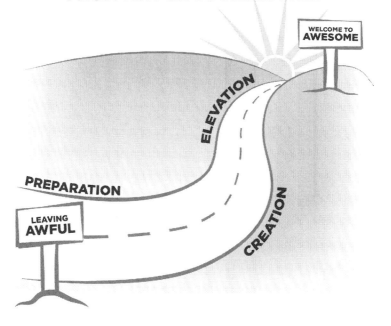

You left "Awful," and traveled on "Presentation Road" to your ultimate destination, "Awesome." Your first stop was at Presentation Preparation, where you picked up those frequently neglected foundational tools for a presentation—Message, Audience and Stage. Next, you continued on your journey to your second stop, Presentation Creation, where you learned how to create the presentation itself using tools that build on each other—Structure, Content, and Delivery. Your final stop before your destination was at Presentation Elevation. There you focused on tools that will further enhance your effectiveness—Review, Rehearsal, and Resources. With some Bonus tools that you found hidden in the trunk, you looked out the window to see the "Welcome to AWESOME" sign—**YOU MADE IT! GREAT JOB!**

By reading this book to the end, you have made a commitment to avoid contributing to the epidemic of awful presentations. On behalf of your future audiences—THANK YOU! I really appreciate your willingness to make each presentation as effective and meaningful as possible—don't squander those opportunities. As a presenter, what you say has value. Now that you know what the nine tools are, you have no excuse for not using them to share that value and insight with others.

In the Introduction, I shared the story of my first, and definitely the worst, presentation that I ever gave. It was a spectacular crash and burn, and it left some scars—I won't lie. I didn't utilize any of the effective presentation tools because I was basically clueless. If you had sat in my audience that day, you would NEVER have believed that one day I would write a book on how to give effective presentations. Fast-forward to today—I recently had an experience that was quite a contrast to that first one. I utilized all of my Presentation Preparation, Presentation Creation, and Presentation Elevation tools, and some from the Bonus section also.

The audience feedback/participation/enthusiasm during the presentation was great. I was feeling pretty good. Then it just got better. One of the participants handed me a folded piece of paper and quickly left. I opened up the note and read, "Thank you for presenting a very educational subject. It was extremely helpful. You are a great speaker!" Wow.

If I can go from Awful to Awesome by using these effective presentation tools—you can too. Buckle up and enjoy the ride!

About the Author

Don Franceschi is a Regional Loss Prevention Manager for the State of California, where he has worked for over 28 years. After sitting through one too many awful presentations, Don decided to quit complaining about the problem and be part of the solution. He has taken his years of practical presentation experience, training, and education, and created a roadmap to guide inexperienced, infrequent, or ineffective business presenters *From Awful to Awesome.*

Don lives in Santa Rosa, California, with his wife Elena and his son Ean. When he is not saving the world from awful presentations, he loves to run, play poker, and vacation in Lake Tahoe.

SPECIAL OFFER

Thank you for buying my book! To show my appreciation, please go to http://www.FromAwfulTo Awesome.com and receive a FREE downloadable workbook to supplement the tools, techniques, and tips discussed in this book.

Included in the FREE workbook are some of the forms, checklists, and chapter summary charts that can help you master those all-important 9 essential tools for effective presentations.

Did I mention the workbook is FREE?

Help support the worthy cause of saving the world from awful presentations!

http://www.FromAwfulToAwesome.com